George Orwell Studies

Volume Eight

No. 2

George Orwell Studies

Publishing Office
Abramis Academic
ASK House
Northgate Avenue
Bury St. Edmunds
Suffolk
IP32 6BB
UK

Tel: +44 (0)1284 717884
Fax: +44 (0)1284 717889
Email: info@abramis.co.uk
Web: www.abramis.co.uk

Copyright
All rights reserved. No part of this publication may be reproduced in any material form (including photocopying or storing it in any medium by electronic means, and whether or not transiently or incidentally to some other use of this publication) without the written permission of the copyright owner, except in accordance with the provisions of the Copyright, Designs and Patents Act 1988, or under terms of a licence issued by the Copyright Licensing Agency Ltd, 33-34, Alfred Place, London WC1E 7DP, UK. Applications for the copyright owner's permission to reproduce part of this publication should be addressed to the Publishers.

© 2024 George Orwell Studies & Abramis Academic

ISSN 2399-1267
ISBN 978-1-84549-834-4

Contents

George Orwell Studies

Editorial
Boom times for the Orwell Industry: A cause for celebration — by Richard Lance Keeble — Page 1

Papers
George Orwell and Somerset Maugham: A comparative study — by Hassan Akram — Page 4
BBC transcript found: 'The meaning of scorched earth' — by Darcy Moore — Page 20

Article
Eileen, '1984' and *Nineteen Eighty-Four* — by John Rodden — Page 32

Interview
George Orwell Studies book reviews' editor Megan Faragher speaks with D.J. Taylor about his latest book, *Orwell: The New Life* — Page 49

Book Reviews
Douglas Kerr on *Beasts of England*, by Adam Biles; Mir Ali Hosseini on *The Socialist Patriot: George Orwell and War*, by Peter Stansky; John Newsinger on *The Never End: The Other Orwell, the Cold War, the CIA, MI6 and the Origin of* Animal Farm, by John Reed; Richard Lance Keeble on *Polymath: The Life and Professions of Dr Alex Comfort, Author of* The Joy of Sex, by Eric Laursen; Megan Faragher on *George Orwell: The Ethics of Equality*, by Peter Brian Barry — Page 63

Review Essay
Wifedom: Fundamentally Flawed — by Richard Lance Keeble — Page 87

And Finally
A new, lively, gossipy column by the appropriately anonymous New Pitcher to intrigue and entertain Orwellians — Page 98

Editors
Richard Lance Keeble — University of Lincoln
Tim Crook — Goldsmiths, University of London

Reviews Editor
Megan Faragher — Wright State University

Production Editor
Paul Anderson — University of Essex

Editorial Board
Kristin Bluemel — Monmouth University, New Jersey
Dorian Lynskey — Author, journalist
Peter Marks — University of Sydney
John Newsinger — Bath Spa University
Marina Remy — Paris Sorbonne
John Rodden — University of Texas at Austin
Jean Seaton — University of Westminster
Peter Stansky — Stanford University, US
D. J. Taylor — Author, journalist, biographer of Orwell
Martin Tyrrell — Queen's University, Belfast
Nathan Waddell — University of Birmingham
Florian Zollmann — Newcastle University

With editorial assistance from Marja Giejgo

Cover image
Lainy Dalzell is an artist originally from Yorkshire who has made her home in Louth, Lincolnshire. Lainy enjoys allowing the subject of her paintings to live within an abstract background without obscuring either. Using a limited palette she enables both subject and background to combine organically.

EDITORIAL

Boom Times for the Orwell Industry: A Cause for Celebration

RICHARD LANCE KEEBLE

The Orwell Industry has never had it so good! Books on the man and his writings are currently being churned out by publishers. The famous author of *Nineteen Eighty-Four* (most of his writings now out of copyright) is clearly a marketable brand out there to be exploited.

Here's a selection of the new texts (many of them covered in *GOS*) featuring both well-established publishing houses and smaller independents: *George Orwell's Perverse Humanity*, by Glenn Burgess (Bloomsbury Academic, 2023), *The Orwell Tour*, by Oliver Lewis (Icon Books, 2023), *Wifedom*, by Anna Funder (Viking, 2023), *Beasts of England*, by Adam Biles (Galley Beggar Press, 2023), *Julia*, by Sandra Newman (Granta, 2023), *Orwell's Island: George, Jura and 1984*, by Les Wilson (Saraband, 2023), *year1984*, by Brennan Conaway (Ministry of Truth, 2023 – and written entirely in newspeak)*, George Orwell: The Ethics of Equality*, by Peter Brian Barry (Oxford University Press, 2023) and *1948: A Critical and Creative Prequel to Orwell's 1984*, by Brian May (University of Exeter Press, 2023). In addition, Constable last year published D.J. Taylor's annotated versions of *Burmese Days* and *A Clergyman's Daughter*.

Orwellian adaptations continue to appear. I'm shortly off to see Hull Truck Theatre Company's adaptation, by Ian Wooldridge, of *Animal Farm*: 'Orwell's enduring and devastating satire about the corruption of power will be brought vividly to life on stage in this compelling drama,' according to the publicity.

A fascinating 'George Talk', organised by The Orwell Society (https://orwellsociety.com/about-the-society/george-talks/), looked in detail at three recent texts: Masha Karp's *George Orwell and Russia* (Bloomsbury Academic, 2023), Sandra Newman's *Julia* and Anna Funder's *Wifedom*. Yet in the lengthy discussion following the presentations only one text was commented on: *Wifedom*. So much is coming out on Orwell these days, it's perhaps impossible to keep up with everything. And Funder's text has certainly gained

RICHARD LANCE KEEBLE

enormous, generally very positive coverage in the corporate media internationally. It's in *The Sunday Times*'s Top Ten list of bestsellers, long-listed for the Women's Prize for Non-Fiction and short-listed for the Gordon Burn Prize. Tom Hanks is even quoted: 'A marvellous book … I just loved it all and have a permanently marked-up, dog-eared copy on my shelf for the next generation.'

Yet, while damning Orwell's misogyny and the persistent patriarchal prejudices of the (all male) biographers, *Wifedom*, in many areas, is fundamentally flawed. Serious errors of fact are being corrected for the second edition.

In an important essay in The Orwell Society *Journal*, No. 23, John Rodden expresses the fear that the reputation of Orwell (forever now labelled a woman-hater) could be seriously damaged in the *Wifedom* fall-out. And in this issue of *George Orwell Studies*, Rodden considers the possible 're-shaping' of the Orwell legacy in the wake of *Wifedom*. I'm optimistic. Amidst the new crop of texts there will, inevitably, be some gems – but also some duds. In recent years, I have felt Richard Bradford's *Orwell: Man of Our Time* (Bloomsbury Caravel, 2020) set a bad precedent since the author used the text simply as a sounding board for many of his (rather eccentric) ideas about Brexit, antisemitism in the Labour Party, the British working class, Trump, Boris Johnson, Downton Abbey and so on. Similarly, in *Orwell's Nose: A Pathological Biography* (Reaktion Books, 2016), while original and entertaining in places, John Sutherland was tempted to fill the gaps in the biography with often tasteless speculation. Yet overall the rapid recent expansion of Orwell Studies, having survived these 'threats', is surely a cause for celebration.

The publication of *Wifedom* – which I also critique in an extended review essay in this issue of *GOS* – has certainly served to expose the serious limitations of the reviewers in the mainstream media.

And, as Glenn Burgess reminds us in his excellent *George Orwell's Perverse Humanity* (2023: 5): 'Giving offence was part of the fun. Orwell *enjoyed* combat with the typewriter; he relished putting his enemies to the verbal sword. He would have had little time for modern sensitivities and our marked (if selective) reluctance to upset others' (italics in the original). Indeed, lively Orwellian debate is at the heart of this journal. Orwell Studies will certainly withstand the *Wifedom* 'combat' and continue to offer still more intriguing insights into the life and writings of Eileen O'Shaughnessy's husband.

Oh, and by the way, still more Orwellian texts are already set for publication this year. They include Paul Theroux's *Burma Sahib* (Hamish Hamilton), Orwell à Paris (Exils), by Duncan Roberts, D.J. Taylor's *Who is Big Brother? A Reader's Guide to George Orwell* (Yale University Press), *The Oxford Handbook of George Orwell* (all 48 chapters edited by Nathan Waddell: Oxford University Press), *George Orwell in Context* (also edited by Nathan Waddell: Cambridge University Press). And the two editors of *George Orwell Studies* are editing a 320,000-word *Routledge Companion to George Orwell*. Happy reading!

Richard Lance Keeble
His most recent publication is Literary Journalism Goes Inside Prison: Just Sentences (Routledge, with David Swick) in which he examines Orwell's attitudes and writings on prisons

PAPER

George Orwell and Somerset Maugham: A Comparative Study

HASSAN AKRAM

For George Orwell, W. Somerset Maugham was 'the modern writer who has influenced me most'. Beyond their shared lucidity of style, there are many thematic connections between Maugham and Orwell's bodies of work. They shared many influences, including Rudyard Kipling, George Gissing and H.G. Wells. Orwell's treatment of themes such as imperialism, the literary world, poverty and nostalgia, all rely on Maugham's model. In this paper I examine three of Orwell's novels through a purely Maughamian lens. Burmese Days *draws on many of Maugham's plots and settings;* Keep the Aspidistra Flying *is a literary satire in the vein of Maugham's* Cakes and Ale; *and* Coming Up For Air *is at least as much a Maughamian novel as a Wellsian one. I end by considering whether Maugham, who outlived Orwell by fifteen years, ever read any of his protégé's work.*

Key words: Orwell, Maugham, influence, colonialism, literary life, poverty

INTRODUCTION

Scholars and critics of Orwell have not paid as much attention to Somerset Maugham's impact on his writing as they have to other influences like D.H. Lawrence or James Joyce, which is strange given that, in Orwell's own words, Maugham was 'the modern writer who has influenced me most… I admire [him] immensely for his power of telling a story straightforwardly and without frills' (*CWGO* XII: 148). One reason for this omission of Maugham may be a desire not to associate Orwell, the greatest writer of his century, with one whose reputation has never been high and who is about as middlebrow as they come. A comparison between Maugham and the author of *Animal Farm* would in most cases be in Orwell's favour. It has not been otherwise since at least 1938, when the journalist Desmond Young called Orwell 'the best writer in England since Somerset Maugham' (Crick 1980: 238).

Maugham's significance should not, of course, be underrated. He had an immeasurable impact on at least three generations of

English literature. With Bernard Shaw, John Galsworthy and H.G. Wells, he was among the most popular Edwardians, and he strongly influenced the inter-war (Orwell, Graham Greene, Evelyn Waugh) and post-war (Ian Fleming, Kingsley Amis, John le Carré) novelists. He continues to shape popular culture – the entire modern espionage genre, for instance, owes much to *Ashenden* (1928) – and he remains relatively widely read both in Europe and in the Asian countries where his most famous stories are set.

To anyone who looks for it, his presence in Orwell's writing is quite clear. They both began their respective careers with accounts of London poverty: *Liza of Lambeth* (1897) and *Down and Out in Paris and London* (1933). Orwell admitted that the model for his own lucid prose style was Maugham's *Ashenden* (Bowker 2010). As early as 1931, he expressed his interest in reviewing any new books by Maugham (*CELJ* 1: 55), and the early short essays, 'A Hanging' (1931) and 'Shooting an Elephant' (1936), appear to have been written under the influence of *On a Chinese Screen* (1922) (Kerr 2022: 55). In some books, he refers to Maugham by name. Several pages of *The Road to Wigan Pier* (1937) are spent analysing Maugham's views on the working class and, in *Keep the Aspidistra Flying* (1936), Gordon Comstock considers going into a cinema to watch the film adaptation of *The Painted Veil* (1934). Orwell's own opinions of Maugham's work are variable. He thought that *Of Human Bondage* (1915), Maugham's masterpiece, was 'stuffed full of literary faults but ... not likely to drop out of favour' (*CEJL* 1: 190). He had warmer words for *Liza of Lambeth*, which 'I happen to have read this year and especially enjoyed – sufficiently to make me want to say to everyone, "Do read this"' (*CWGO* XVIII: 8).

More significantly, there are thematic traces of Maugham scattered across Orwell's work as a novelist. Their novels are complementary when read alongside each other, and they share many of the same themes and influences. *Burmese Days* (1934), *Keep the Aspidistra Flying* (1936) and *Coming Up For Air* (1939) bear the influence most strongly, though they have rarely been looked at from a purely Maughamian point of view, which is the aim of this paper.

BURMESE DAYS

Maugham's influence is most apparent in Orwell's first novel. This is true of the book's Eastern locales and theme of colonialism, but goes down even to basic structural aspects such as character and plot.

For instance, the entire triangle between John Flory, Elizabeth Lackersteen and Ma Hla May is lifted from one of Maugham's short stories. 'The Force of Circumstance' (1924) is about a colonial officer, Guy, whose marriage to an Englishwoman ends when she discovers his previous affair with a Malaysian woman, just as Flory's marriage to Elizabeth Lackersteen is averted by her disgust at discovering his past affair with Ma Hla May. The parallel is so clear that Orwell most likely had the story in mind when he wrote *Burmese Days*.

The relationship between Flory and Elizabeth themselves is even more notable for having been taken straight out of Maugham's *Of Human Bondage*. Maugham explains in his preface that *Of Human Bondage* is for the most part an autobiography and that its hero, Philip, is a self-portrait like Orwell's Flory. The most memorable part of the book is the account of Philip's affair with Mildred Rogers, a waitress-turned-prostitute. Mildred is shown to be vulgar, narrow-minded and snobbish; she has nothing in common with Philip yet, despite her being unfaithful and using him for her own goals, he is infatuated by her. The same outline may just as accurately summarise the Flory-Elizabeth romance, which traces exactly the same course as the Philip-Mildred one. Flory's 'hideous birthmark stretching in a ragged crescent down his left cheek' (Orwell 2001 [1934]: 14) is almost certainly a rendering of Philip's clubfoot. The difference, of course, is that the clubfoot is lifted from life (it was based on Maugham's own disabling stammer) whereas Flory's scar is lifted from Maugham. Clubfoot and scar nonetheless perform the same function in that both Philip and Flory suffer from self-consciousness and self-loathing and that, just as Mildred ultimately deserts Philip by jeering that he is a 'cripple!'(2000 [1915]: 552), so in Elizabeth's eyes it was, finally, 'the birthmark that had damned' Flory (2001 [1934]: 290).

It is unclear whether Orwell was paying homage to Maugham or if he meant Flory as a sort of creative reimagining. What is certain from the characters and relationships in *Burmese Days* is that he relies too much on Maugham's model. It cannot be a good thing that he transposes entire characters and relationships from another novel into his own. His likely reason for doing so was that characters and feelings were secondary to his main aim of delivering a political message. It is when he does deliver that message – which in *Burmese Days* is one about British colonialism – that he goes far beyond Maugham.

By way of an introduction to Maugham and Orwell's treatment of colonialism, it is worth quoting a passage from Douglas Kerr's book *Orwell & Empire* (2022: 11):

> Somerset Maugham travelled widely in Asia, a professional writer in search of copy. He is also probably the strongest literary presence in Orwell's Burmese writing. ... Maugham is uninterested in making political judgements, but beady-eyed

in his observation of the Anglo-Indians (and Anglo-Malayans), with what Orwell called 'a kind of stoical resignation, the stiff upper lip of the pukka sahib somewhere East of Suez, carrying on with his job without believing in it, like an Antonine Emperor'.

The important point here is that 'Maugham is uninterested in making political judgements'. This deserves to be examined at greater length because political judgements are exactly what Orwell *is* interested in making. *Burmese Days* demonstrates both a ruthless disgust at British colonialism and a thorough grasp of it – informed by Orwell's 'wasted years' in the Imperial Police force. He saw through the nineteenth-century myths, exemplified by the work of Kipling, about 'enlightened despotism' and a 'civilising mission'; and his contempt for that worldview explains why, in *Burmese Days*, almost every aspect of the colonial system is observed and attacked.

In an earlier article he had written that 'if Burma derives some incidental benefit from the English, she must pay dearly for it. … Their relationship with the British Empire is that of slave and master' (*CWGO* X: 147). Post-colonial critics would find little to dispute here. In the novel he re-words the same point: 'The Indian Empire is a despotism – benevolent, no doubt, but still a despotism with theft as its final object' (Orwell 2001 [1934]: 68). He emphasises, moreover, the role of racial hierarchies in cementing an 'us-and-them' divide ('Remember, we are *sahiblog* and they are dirt', ibid: 198); and, foreshadowing doublethink of *Nineteen Eighty-Four*, he records some of the hypocrisies of the colonial mindset: 'Provided they were given no freedom he thought them the most charming people alive' (ibid: 28). And, when Ellis claims that the Burmese have been 'slaves since the beginning of history' (ibid: 22), it shows an understanding of the self-justifying tactic, historically used against colonised nations, of denying the existence of their cultural heritage. Orwell knew what he was talking about: in 1944, when John Middleton Murry used the same tactic in an article on China, Orwell responded to him saying that 'exactly the same argument ('these people are used to being conquered anyway')… was always brought forward to justify our own rule in India' (*CEJL* 3: 217). Finally there is no mistaking his sense of imperial disillusionment in a passage like: 'Your whole life is a life of lies. Year after year you sit in Kipling-haunted little Clubs, whisky to right of you, Pink'un to left of you, listening and eagerly agreeing while Colonel Bodger develops his theory that these bloody Nationalists should be boiled in oil' (Orwell 2001 [1934]: 69).

Orwell's nonchalance about it all is particularly noteworthy. Even if, at times, the injustice or hypocrisy angers him, he is rarely

PAPER

shocked by it, and his attitude is always essentially detached. 'No Anglo-Indian will ever deny that India is going to the dogs,' he says bluntly (ibid: 27). He is unsurprised. Now, compare this attitude to that in any one of Maugham's colonial stories – 'Rain' (1921), for example, which is the most famous one. Orwell had read this story and, in various articles, he listed it as one of the prime examples of a good short story (*CWGO* XII: 372). It concerns a missionary on an island colony whose aim is to 'civilise' the natives by expunging what he regards as their primitive dance rituals and improper dress. One day, Miss Thompson, a socialite, moves into his guesthouse; the missionary is disgusted by her dress, her music, her parties, and he claims that she is spreading sin. Over time, he grows increasingly obsessed with the idea of reforming her; he devotes himself to the task, meets her and tries to show her the light. Eventually, he seems to have succeeded and she becomes repentant. But then, one morning, the missionary is discovered dead by his own hand and Miss Thompson, on being asked by a doctor what happened, shouts: 'You men! You filthy, dirty pigs! You're all the same, all of you' (Maugham 1963 [1951]: 45). Maugham never tells us outright what has happened, though the implication is clear enough. The point is that he uses the missionary's hypocrisy as a shocker, an unexpected plot twist. Compare this to *Burmese Days*, where hypocrisy is calmly taken for granted, and one can gauge the overall difference in Orwell and Maugham's outlooks. Maugham, who after all began his career in the 1890s at the height of jingo fever, still has the capacity to be shocked at the reality of colonialism – a capacity which Orwell lacked.

Yet although 'Rain' can be interpreted as an attack on colonialism, it may just as plausibly be an attack on religion, or prudishness or simply human nature. Indeed, Maugham's real focus in the story is less on political structures and more on the characters themselves, and he shows a naturalistic concern with their behaviours, environment and instincts. The emphasis on characters over politics – the total opposite of Orwell – is representative of his wider body of work. In his early novels, he throws in a few Conservative MPs here and there, and in his war memoir *Strictly Personal* (1941) he spends a chapter praising the Labour Party. But other than that, he is utterly apolitical and this neutrality extends to his treatment of colonialism. He does not see it as anything more than a good backdrop for telling a story. Another good example of this attitude comes in *Of Human Bondage,* when he uses the Boer War as a key plot point. He takes no sides and offers no comment on the war itself. It is merely a fact, and one which, by bankrupting the hero, drives the story forward. There are countless other examples: *East of Suez* (1922), *The Narrow Corner* (1932) and most of the short stories, all use colonial themes without betraying a shred of political consciousness. From all these examples it becomes clear that his concern is not with institutions nor systems at all. His only consistent aim is to explore 'human nature'.

Orwell's intention, on the other hand, was always to deliver a political message. In 'Why I write' he said that *Animal Farm* was his first conscious attempt 'to fuse political purpose and artistic purpose into one whole' (*CWGO* XVIII: 320) when in every one of his previous novels he had already been doing so. In *Burmese Days*, even when he seems to be dealing with 'human nature', there is a clear political target. Take the character of Ellis. In giving Ellis those viscerally racist monologues, in describing his bloodthirst to massacre crowds and in showing him strike a boy blind, Orwell was not simply drawing a character; he was drawing a microcosm of the very worst kind of colonial officer. Note that Ellis is introduced as 'one of those Englishmen – common, unfortunately – who should never be allowed to set foot in the East': that he is only '*one*' of a '*common*' type. Now, compare Ellis to any similar character of Maugham's: say, Izzard in 'The Yellow Streak' (1925). Izzard is also a colonial officer and a bigot, though not so extreme a one as Ellis. Maugham's only concern with him is character: motivations and psychology. The remarkable thing about this story is that Maugham does not so much as hint at the bigger picture, at the fact that Izzard represents a broader problem, or at the system which upholds his prejudices. He merely uses a dramatic incident in a tidal wave to unpack Izzard's insecurities and trace them to their psychological root. Again, unlike Orwell, in writing this story of prejudice and violence, he is not actually attacking the colonial system.

Indeed, he does not even seem to understand it, and this is his principal weakness as a colonial writer. An anti-imperialist like Orwell – or even a jingo like Kipling – at any rate understood the nature of the system he described, whereas Maugham has no grasp of it at all. His bland view of the Empire, which he gives in his Burmese travelogue *The Gentleman in the Parlour* (1930b), is simply that it 'will have been in the world's history a moment not without grandeur' (2000 [1930b]: 11). Still, it is to the credit of a friend, admirer and few years' junior of Kipling that he nowhere shows any sign of being a jingo-imperialist in the crude sense. It is interesting that in his introduction to *A Choice of Kipling's Prose* (1952), Maugham was able to mention Indian independence as a simple fact, without any emotion or regret; whereas Kipling himself, had he lived until 1947, would have been horrified. But then again, Maugham does not seriously *object* to Kipling's worldview either, at least not as strongly as Orwell does in his *Horizon* essay 'Rudyard Kipling' of 1942 (*CWGO* XIII: 150-162). Maugham is really neither a jingo-imperialist nor an anti-colonialist. He regards the Empire as nothing more than a fact of life, like unemployment or the weather.

One reason for the difference between him and Orwell is that of generation. For a man born in 1874, the Empire simply *would* be a fact of life; while for one born in 1903, the myth had begun to crumble. The difference in outlook was not, of course, purely generational. Orwell's experiences as a colonial officer gave him an insider's perspective which Maugham, a traveller at his leisure, ultimately lacked. Only on tiny details – which are really nothing more than the basic instincts of a traveller – do Maugham and Orwell's outlooks align. For instance, in *Burmese Days*, Westfield's remark that: 'God! What'd you give to be in Piccadilly now, eh?' (2001 [1934]: 37), mirrors an almost identical remark in Maugham's short story 'The Pool', in which a Samoan official longs for the bustle of Piccadilly Circus. These common feelings, along with their shared love of foreign travel and culture, are all they have in common.

As a summing-up, I will end this section with two anecdotes. When *Burmese Days* was published, it 'sparked controversy for its scathing portrayal of colonial society' (ibid: cover blurb) and it had to be published first in America, where it was found to be more palatable. Maugham's *The Painted Veil* (1925), which is set partly in Hong Kong, also caused a libel scandal. This was because the main character, by complete chance, shared the name of some Assistant Colonial Secretary, who felt himself personally attacked and raised hell until Maugham agreed to withdraw the novel and change the names (2000 [1925]: x). This contrast summarises better than anything else the difference between Orwell and Maugham's treatments of the British Empire. Between them is all the difference between a frivolous storyteller and a serious polemicist.

KEEP THE ASPIDISTRA FLYING

In both *Cakes and Ale* (1930a) and *Keep the Aspidistra Flying*, the London literary world is attacked. Maugham's energetic satire is set for the most part in high-end literary circles. Narrated by a writer who is essentially Maugham himself, it is centred on caricatures of Thomas Hardy ('Edward Driffield') and Hugh Walpole ('Alroy Kear'), and its main theme is the relationship – if any – between literary merit, popularity and reputation. When published the novel caused an uproar. 'Trampling on Hardy's grave', one headline ran in response, and Hugh Walpole reportedly burst into tears on recognising himself, though Maugham emerged from the controversies as the best respected novelist in England (Shakespeare 2000: xii-xviii).

The main theme of both Orwell and Maugham's novels – literary life – is the same, though there is an obvious overall difference in tone and perspective. *Cakes and Ale* was written in Maugham's southern French villa; *Aspidistra* was churned out as a potboiler while Orwell was 'half-starved' and 'desperate for money' (*CWGO* XVIII: 411). One is a lively and elegant satire; the other is a blunt and indiscriminate attack.

The books themselves reveal much about their own origin. Orwell observes in *Aspidistra* that a good novel can only be written in propitious circumstances: 'Invention, energy, wit, style, charm – they've all got to be paid for in hard cash' (2000 [1936]: 8). Orwell thought that *Aspidistra* lacked most of these qualities. *Cakes and Ale*, on the other hand, brims with them because Maugham had the 'hard cash', as he explains in the preface to his *Collected Plays*:

> I am not such a fool as to pretend that I am indifferent to the money I have made. Unlike some of my fellow-writers I had no other means of earning a living than my pen. ... Nothing is so degrading as a constant anxiety about means of livelihood. ... Money is like a sixth sense without which one cannot make a complete use of the other five. Without an adequate income half the possibilities of the world are cut off. The only thing to be careful of is that one does not pay more than twenty shillings for the pound one earns (1969 [1952]: xvii).

It is clear from this passage that he had, at some point, experienced the kinds of literary and financial struggles that Orwell describes. Much of Maugham's earlier work did look at poverty, and *Aspidistra* – with the penniless hero, tramping round London in the cold, refusing the help of friends, gaining the love and sympathy of a woman, getting her pregnant and eventually giving up his ambitions in favour of married life and wage slavery – is really a full-length version of what Maugham did in a few chapters at the end of *Of Human Bondage*. Yet Maugham's joke at the end of the passage above makes it equally clear that, once he was financially secure and his reputation had been established, those early experiences no longer affected him. That is probably also why, in *Cakes and Ale*, he has such an optimistic view of his own profession, and at one point he happily elaborates on the perks of being a writer:

> I began to meditate upon the writer's life. ... Whenever he has anything on his mind, whether it be a harassing reflection, grief at the death of a friend, unrequited love, wounded pride, anger at the treachery of someone to whom he has shown kindness, in short any emotion or any perplexing thought, he has only to put it down in black and white, using it as the

theme of a story or the decoration of an essay, to forget all about it. He is the only free man (2000 [1930a]: 195-196).

Orwell's view of novel-writing, which is implicit throughout *Aspidistra* and explicit in his letters and essays, could not be more different:

> I am so miserable, struggling in the entrails of that dreadful book and never getting any further. Never start writing novels, if you wish to preserve your happiness (*CEJL* 1: 160).

> Writing a book is a horrible, exhausting struggle, like a long bout of some painful illness. One would never undertake such a thing if one were not driven on by some demon whom one can neither resist nor understand (ibid: 29).

The reason for the difference in outlook is poverty, which does not appear at all in *Cakes and Ale*, but which drives the whole plot of *Aspidistra*. Indeed, contemporary reviewers focused more on its status as 'a completely harrowing and stark account of *poverty*' (Meyers 1975: 67, emphasis added) rather than on what it had to say about the literary world. Much of the detail is drawn from Orwell's own experiences. However, the general themes of the book – the loathing of commercialism, the idealised view of the past, the conviction that money corrupts human relationships and 'the futility, the bloodiness, the deathliness of modern life' (op cit: 92) – align him not so much with Maugham as with another writer altogether: George Gissing.

Gissing had practically invented the serious 'struggling writer' genre in 1891 with *New Grub Street*. Maugham and Orwell were both, in their ways, successors to him and the connection between the trio is worth examining. *Aspidistra* is so stuffed with Gissingian ideas and themes that, on reading it, Anthony Powell urged Orwell that 'the Gissing had to stop' (Taylor 2024). To give only one example, regarding the theme of money: Orwell says that the commonest phrase in the Comstock household was: 'We can't afford it' (op cit: 42); and this phrase parallels the 'not enough money' which he believed to have been the defining statement of Gissing's novels (*CWGO* XV: 45-47). Maugham, too, was influenced by Gissing, and his early novel *The Merry-Go-Round* (1905) draws heavily on *New Grub Street* in describing the financial, literary and domestic struggles of a novelist who marries 'beneath him'. Even as early as 1905, however, his portrayal is brought down by the fact that he, a successful writer, cannot fully empathise with the struggles of an unsuccessful one (Akram 2024 forthcoming).

There are also similarities between Maugham and Orwell's styles of novel-writing. There is a definite anti-modernist strain in Maugham.

There is reason to think that he was uncomfortable with post-1918 literary modernism and the elitist ideology of Bloomsbury, and at heart he was always an Edwardian writer. After all, his first nine novels were written before 1914; and his best novels from after that date – *Of Human Bondage, The Moon and Sixpence, The Painted Veil, Cakes and Ale, The Razor's Edge* – all follow a traditional style and structure with no modernist experiments, and are all set either before 1914 or in a foreign country. Whenever he wrote about contemporary Britain – as in *Theatre* (1937) – the results were mediocre (though it would still have been interesting to see the post-war London working-class novel which he planned in the 1940s but never wrote) (1949: 321). It may well be that he rejected modernist development because his traditional style had brought him a level of popularity and wealth, which he was not prepared to abandon for the sake of being a literary pioneer. Orwell would also stick to conventional over modernist forms of storytelling (except perhaps in Chapter 3 of *A Clergyman's Daughter*), and he, like Maugham, can never really be considered a pioneering modernist writer. However much he admired James Joyce and the other modernists, he did not use his own style to advance or develop the novel as a literary form. Even the styles of *Animal Farm* and *Nineteen Eighty-Four* were modelled respectively on Jonathan Swift and H.G. Wells rather than being newly developed or unique.

Despite sharing these themes, influences and styles, the gulf between Maugham and Orwell's perspectives remains marked throughout both *Cakes and Ale* and *Aspidistra*. When Maugham writes: 'You feel ill at ease when your friend tells you that his books don't sell and that he can't place his short stories' (2000 [1930a]: 34), he is anticipating Orwell's point that it is difficult for Gordon to get his work published, but he is doing so with a magnanimous, back-seat point of view which is more like that of Gordon's wealthy editor friend Ravelston.

Moreover, as Maugham was emphatically a popular writer, his entire novel is a defence of the popular against the elite in literature. In lines such as 'The elect sneer at popularity; they are inclined even to assert that it is a proof of mediocrity' (ibid: 9), there is a detectable personal bitterness against the fact that (as he would reflect in his memoir *The Summing Up*) 'there are but two important critics in my own country who have troubled to take me seriously' (1963 [1938]: 143). He tries to get his own back at 'the elect', and reminds them 'that posterity makes its choice not from among the unknown writers of a period, but from among the known' (2000 [1930a]: 91). Here again is a difference of perspective between him and Orwell. In *Aspidistra*, Orwell does not defend popular writers. Far from it, he reserves the worst of his mockery for lowbrows of the

Edgar Wallace/Ethel M. Dell type, while making an effort to stick up for unsuccessful writers like Gordon. By defending his own kind of writer (the 'unknown') and disparaging the rest, he is doing the same as Maugham did in *Cakes and Ale*, the difference being that he and Maugham are in opposite positions.

Surprisingly, however, Maugham and Orwell focus their satire on identical targets. There is an interesting passage in which Maugham mentions that 'The wise always use a number of ready-made phrases... [to] avoid the necessity of thought' (ibid: 23), which foreshadows almost to the letter Orwell's criticism, in 'Politics and the English Language' (1946), of the use of hackneyed phrases to prevent thought. They are also united in their loathing of 'the extinct monsters of the Victorian age' (2000 [1936]: 7) and, when Orwell moans that 'Carlyle and Ruskin and Meredith and Stevenson – are all dead, God rot them' (ibid: 9), he is exactly echoing Maugham's quip that 'Meredith has gone all to pot, and Carlyle was a pretentious windbag' (2000 [1930a]: 27). Also identical is their loathing of literary pretension and of bad writers masquerading as good ones. It is significant that *Aspidistra*'s Mrs Penn, the middlebrow customer who is observed with detached sarcasm, claims that 'Now, [Hugh] Walpole, you know, I consider a really great writer' (2000 [1936]: 11). In choosing Hugh Walpole of all writers to burn at effigy, Orwell is almost certainly imitating Maugham. They picked their target well, because Walpole was the prime example of a bad writer held up as a good one. (The decline of his reputation since his death in 1941 tells its own story: barely any of his four-dozen books remain in print today, while ninety-year-old copies of them are ten a penny in every second-hand bookshop in London.)

Unlike Maugham, however, Orwell does not examine *why* it is that so many celebrated writers are unreadable. He is merely ranting and, what is more, he is self-aware enough to see the futility of his own position. Like Gordon in Chapter 8, he is 'being witty at the expense of modern literature' but is doing so 'with the fine scorn of the unpublished' and using only 'a careless phrase or two' (ibid: 178). The self-awareness of these descriptions indicates his knowledge that, however many insults he throws at Ethel M. Dell, she will not even read them, let alone be reduced to tears by them.

Compare this to Maugham's novel, where the satire is not only witty but is effective in hitting its target. Maugham does not simply call Walpole a bad writer; he draws a book-length caricature of him as a talentless sycophant who sucks up to reviewers and lauds the men of the moment. He explains exactly *how* bad writers can pose as good ones. Orwell does this up to a point, using his inverted Etonian snobbery to criticise the elite university networks that allow 'moneyed young beasts ... [to] glide gracefully from Eton to

Cambridge and from Cambridge to the literary reviews' (ibid: 7) just as Maugham hints that Alroy Kear only became successful through the connections he gained as president of the Oxford Union. But Orwell's comment is just a side note; his real criticism is reserved for social and political topics rather than literary ones. Overall, he remains too constrained by personal circumstances, and too reliant on pre-existing targets, to create caricatures or write a literary satire of the calibre of *Cakes and Ale*, which – for its invention, energy, wit, style and charm – is probably the superior novel.

COMING UP FOR AIR

H.G. Wells must have been one of the very few people who knew both Maugham and Orwell (and, for that matter, George Gissing). In 1941, Orwell wrote 'Wells, Hitler and the World State' (*CWGO* XII: 536-541), in which he argued that Wells, despite having shaped the thinking of the entire generation born between 1900 and 1920, had become an anachronism, and had been repeating the same worn-out lines for decades. In the same year, Maugham met Wells in New York and made some remarks almost identical to Orwell's:

> [Wells] couldn't understand why they [the general public] were impatient with him for saying very much the same sort of thing that he had been saying for thirty years. ... One would have thought it was enough for H.G. to reflect on the great influence he had on a whole generation and how much he did to alter the climate of opinion (1949: 276).

I mention this, firstly because it is interesting that Maugham's and Orwell's perspectives on a single writer should align so perfectly, and secondly because *Coming Up For Air* owes a great deal to Wells's middle-class comedies, *Kipps* (1905) and *The History of Mr Polly* (1910). Orwell considered that Wells's 'greatest gift, although he has never realised it, was his power to convey the atmosphere of the golden years between 1890 and 1914' (*CWGO* XII: 191) and in his last pre-war novel Orwell tries to recapture the atmosphere of those very years. The book's main theme is nostalgia. Through his hero George Bowling, Orwell examines his own personal fascination with the Edwardian period: the 'never-never land' that people are thinking of when they say before the war' (2000 [1939]: 35).

Significantly, Orwell's own point of view is that of one who grew up in the Edwardian era. His memories of it are tinged by nostalgia, and he imbues it with a feeling of otherworldliness. This places his perspective at odds with that of Maugham who, in the same era, would already have been a grown man and who best conveyed his view of the period in one of his short stories. In 'The Voice of the Turtle' (1935), a *Cakes and Ale*-style narrator adopts a literary protégé, a debutant who wants to set his new novel 'in the beginning of the Edwardian era, which to the young has already acquired the fantastic, far-away feeling of a past age' (1963 [1951]: 252). There is an obvious generational divide here, and Maugham's view of 'the young' shows a kind of detachment. It seems to strike him as very comic that young writers should imbue the 1900s with that 'fantastic, far-away feeling', and, if only *Coming Up For Air* had been written a few years earlier, it would have been tempting to read this young novelist character as a stand-in for Orwell.

It is in *Cakes and Ale* that Maugham explores the theme of nostalgia most seriously. Woven in with the literary sections of the novel are the narrator's memories of his Victorian childhood. These chapters have the same hazy quality as the parallel ones in *Coming Up For Air*, though, tellingly, Maugham does not idealise the past as much as Orwell does. In fact, he does the opposite, saying that 'I fancy life is more amusing now than it was forty years ago and I have a notion that people are more amiable' (2000 [1930a]: 32). Although one would not know if from reading the first half of *Coming Up For Air*, Orwell agreed with him on this point. Across Orwell's essays there is a clear sense that, in terms of living standards and social norms, 'the present age is a good deal better than the last one' (*CEJL* 4: 484). He knows in his heart that to romanticise the Edwardians is to gloss over all sorts of terrible things, but, as *Coming Up For Air* demonstrates, he cannot resist reminiscing fondly about them.

The final chapters of *Coming Up For Air* are so similar to those of *Cakes and Ale* that it becomes difficult to see them as anything but a copy-and-paste job. In both novels the narrator returns to the village of his childhood, which was detailed earlier on, and walks around reflecting on how much everything has changed. There is the same clash between old memories and encroaching modernity ('the stationery shop where I had bought paper and wax to make rubbings ... was unchanged; there were two or three cinemas and their garish posters', Maugham 2000 [1930a]: 169); and the same brooding over the churchyard graves ('Gann was one of the commonest names at Blackstable. The churchyard was thick with their graves', ibid: 57). One moment in particular, when Maugham's narrator approaches a barman to tell 'him my name, in the days of his boyhood better known than any other at Blackstable, but somewhat to my mortification I saw that it aroused no echo in his memory' (ibid: 169), is repeated almost exactly in Orwell's novel when Bowling, in the hope of being recognised, gives his name to a barmaid, who has 'Never heard of George Bowling, son of Samuel Bowling – Samuel Bowling who, damn it! had had his half-pint in this same pub every Saturday for over thirty years' (2000 [1939]: 196).

The important point about Orwell's final scenes is that they deflate the sense of nostalgia which had been built up earlier on. They bring Bowling back to the present and prepare him to face what had previously been an uncomfortable future of war and totalitarianism. Maugham is more indulgent. He chooses to end his novel with a happy flashback, so in the end he is not as fierce as Orwell in renouncing nostalgia.

CONCLUSION

Christopher Hitchens – one of Orwell's greatest admirers and closest imitators – loathed Somerset Maugham. In his essay 'Poor Old Willie' (2004), he demolishes the remains of Maugham's reputation, complaining that the plots are tired and the characters dull, and that his 'overall debt to Conrad is so evident that one usually finishes by putting him down and picking the real thing up' (though on this point the same could really be said about Hitchens's debt to Orwell). Hitchens is especially vitriolic in attacking what he regards as Maugham's clichéd and clumsy writing style. As a justification for his contempt, he quotes a passage from *Ashenden* – ironically the very book which Orwell used for himself as a style guide (see Bowker 2010). Orwell once said: 'There are some writers whose line of literary descent is so clear as to remind one of those chapters of the Old Testament which consist entirely of "and so-and-so". Thus, Cervantes begat Smollett, and Smollett begat Dickens...' (see Lethbridge 2024). Likewise, Maugham begat Orwell and Orwell begat Hitchens, and this line of descent makes Hitchens's hatred even more perplexing.

The fact is that Hitchens represents a broader celebration of Orwell which utterly neglects Maugham. Up to a point this is justified for, after all, Maugham was not a 'great' writer like Orwell. Yet, as I have tried to show, Maugham's and Orwell's novels share many of the same themes (imperialism, literature, poverty, nostalgia) and influences (Kipling, Gissing, Wells), and they complement each other when read side-by-side. *Burmese Days* borrows some of Maugham's character relationships but goes beyond him in an uncompromising attack on the British Empire. *Keep the Aspidistra Flying* is a blunter version of *Cakes and Ale*, though it offers far more in the way of political and social commentary. *Coming Up For Air* is also a self-consciously Maughamian novel, but in the end it is less nostalgic and more realistic than Maugham in facing a potentially dystopian future.

There is only one facet of the Maugham-Orwell relationship that remains unknown. Did Maugham ever read Orwell? And, if so, was he aware that he was reading the work of one of his protégés? Maugham burned all his papers in a bonfire a few years before he died and in his published articles there is no mention of Orwell. If there remains any way of throwing light on this question, it may be of more value in understanding the connection between the pair than anything else I have highlighted.

REFERENCES

Akram, Hassan (2024, forthcoming) George Gissing and Somerset Maugham, *The Gissing Journal*, July

Bowker, Gordon (2010) Orwell's Library. Available online at https://www.orwellfoundation.com/the-orwell-foundation/orwell/articles/gordon-bowker-orwells-library/, accessed on 3 February 2024

Crick, Bernard (1980) *George Orwell: A Life*, Boston: Little, Brown

Hitchens, Christopher (2004) Poor Old Willie, *The Atlantic*, May. Available online at https://www.theatlantic.com/magazine/archive/2004/05/poor-old-willie/302935/, accessed on 3 February 2024

Kerr, Douglas (2022) *Orwell & Empire*, Oxford: Oxford University Press

Lethbridge, John P. (2024) Walpoling activities, orwellsociety.com, 24 January. Available online at https://orwellsociety.com/walpoling-activities/, accessed on 3 February 2024

Maugham, W. Somerset (2000 [1915]) *Of Human Bondage*, London: Vintage

Maugham, W. Somerset (2000 [1925]) *The Painted Veil*, London: Vintage

Maugham, W. Somerset (2000 [1930a]) *Cakes and Ale*, London: Vintage

Maugham, W. Somerset (2000 [1930b]) *The Gentleman in the Parlour*, London: Vintage

Maugham, W. Somerset (1963 [1938]) *The Summing Up*, Harmondsworth, Middlesex: Penguin Books

Maugham, W. Somerset (1949) *A Writer's Notebook*, London: William Heinemann

Maugham, W. Somerset (1963 [1951]) *Collected Short Stories, Vol. 1*, Harmondsworth, Middlesex: Penguin

Maugham, W. Somerset (1969 [1952]) *The Collected Plays, Vol. 1*, London: Heron Books

Meyers, Jeffrey (ed.) (1975) *George Orwell: The Critical Heritage*, London: Routledge

Orwell, George [2001 (1934)] *Burmese Days*, London: Penguin

Orwell, George (2000 [1936]) *Keep the Aspidistra Flying*, London: Penguin Books

Orwell, George (2000 [1939]) *Coming Up For Air*, London: Penguin Books

Orwell, George (1968) *The Collected Essays, Journalism and Letters, Vols 1, 2 and 4*, Harmondsworth, Middlesex: Penguin

Orwell, George (1998) *The Complete Works of George Orwell: (CWGO), XX Vols.*, London: Secker & Warburg

Shakespeare, Nicholas (2000) Introduction, Maugham, W. Somerset (2000 [1930a]) *Cakes and Ale*, London: Vintage

Taylor, D.J. (2024) In praise of George Gissing, the born exile, *The Spectator World*, 23 January. Available online at https://thespectator.com/book-and-art/george-gissing-born-exile/, accessed on 3 February 2024

NOTE ON THE CONTRIBUTOR

Hassan Akram is a student and a writer of short stories and essays. In 2018, he picked up a worn copy of *Nineteen Eighty-Four* and he has been a devoted Orwell fan ever since. He has written essays on other topics for publications such as *The Gissing Journal,* and his fiction has also appeared in places such as *Humour Me Magazine*. He is currently studying at the University of Oxford, where he is a regular contributor and editor on *Cherwell*.

PAPER

PAPER

BBC Transcript Found: 'The Meaning of Scorched Earth'

DARCY MOORE

George Orwell was employed in the Indian Section of the BBC's Eastern Service during World War Two from 1941-1943. Although many radio scripts from the 1940s have been lost, there is an almost complete record of Programmes as Broadcast (PasB) which provides an invaluable inventory of what was transmitted. Here, Darcy Moore tells of how, during a recent six-week research trip to India, he discovered a long-lost transcript of a talk given by Orwell on the BBC in January 1942.

Key words: Orwell, BBC Eastern Service, scorched earth

My lengthy list of ideas to pursue, people and sites to visit, including archives and libraries, was never going to be ticked-off in one six-week research trip to India. Locating primary sources that broaden our understanding of Orwell's complex relationship with his Anglo-Indian heritage and learning from local historians in Motihari (where he was born) and Nainital (where his parents married) kept me busy for most of the time.

Besides finding out more about Orwell's parents and his extended family who had lived and worked in India, there were many other incidental byways to be explored. Some may be considered a little unlikely or even quixotic – but nevertheless were important by my estimation. Could Orwell's ayah (nursemaid) be identified or was this unknown woman truly lost to history (Moore 2023)? Did Orwell's mother leave India with her children after her son was bitten in his cot by a rat (Moore 2022)? On the last full-day researching in the archives, one of these longer research shots – pertaining to Orwell's many Indian colleagues at the BBC – hit an unlikely bullseye.

Peter Davison, editor of the *Complete Works*, had noted a PasB record for 15 January 1942 which had not survived: 'The Meaning of Scorched Earth' written by E. Blair and read by Balraj Sahni (Orwell 1998 [1941-1942]: 121). There was a small lead contained in a letter to Mulk Raj Anand (1905-2004), written shortly afterwards, on 27 February 1942 and signed 'Eric Blair', indicating that Orwell posted exemplar transcripts of BBC broadcasts to prospective speakers as 'guidance copies':

> Dear Anand,
>
> I wonder if you would like to do a series of talks on Sundays, which would mean recording the talks normally on Fridays? I recently wrote myself two talks explaining what is meant by scorched earth and by sabotage, and it afterwards occurred to me that as we have about five Sundays vacant, we might have a series, discussing similar phrases which have passed into general usage in the last year or two, and are flung to and fro in newspaper articles, broadcasts and so forth, without necessarily being well understood.
>
> I would like you, if you would, to do these talks, starting with one on the phrase Fifth Column, and following up with talks discussing propaganda, living space, new order, pluto-democracy, racialism, and so on. I am sending you as sort of guidance copies of the first two talks I did. You will see from these that our idea is to make these catch-phrases more intelligible, and at the same time, of course, to do a bit of anti-Fascist propaganda. Could you let me know pretty soon whether this would interest you?
>
> Yours
>
> Eric Blair
>
> Talks Assistant
>
> Indian Section (ibid: 192).

The National Archives of India in New Delhi is home to a large collection of Mulk Raj Anand's private papers. Could these transcripts be located among the writer's literary estate? It was worth an hour or two of precious archival time to see what was still extant. Eureka! The pages were fragile, frayed and browning, a few words were illegible and it was slightly truncated – but the 'guidance' copy Orwell had slipped into an envelope over 80 years ago had survived! I excitedly read, photographed, endeavoured to faithfully copy the text without correcting typos, counted word length and considered the broadcast time, comparing it with other scripts. It seemed complete, except for the last few words, or possibly paragraphs which may have been on a discarded third page.

THE MEANING OF SCORCHED EARTH

Anyone who listened to this broadcast in mid-January 1942 was thoroughly and rationally briefed about the concept of 'scorched earth' across several theatres of war (Orwell 1942a). The tone is appropriately dispassionate, as a police officer would report on the violent murder of a citizen in neutral, unemotive language. Orwell correctly identified that the term scorched earth was first used in a report made during the Second Sino-Japanese War (1937-1945) but it is odd he does not mention to his audience that this concept had been employed militarily since antiquity. It is noticeable, considering this text was read aloud for radio, that Orwell erred a little – probably due to the hurly-burly of relentlessly having to prepare content for broadcast – in the first sentence of the second last paragraph by writing, 'as I noted above' rather than something like, 'as already mentioned'.

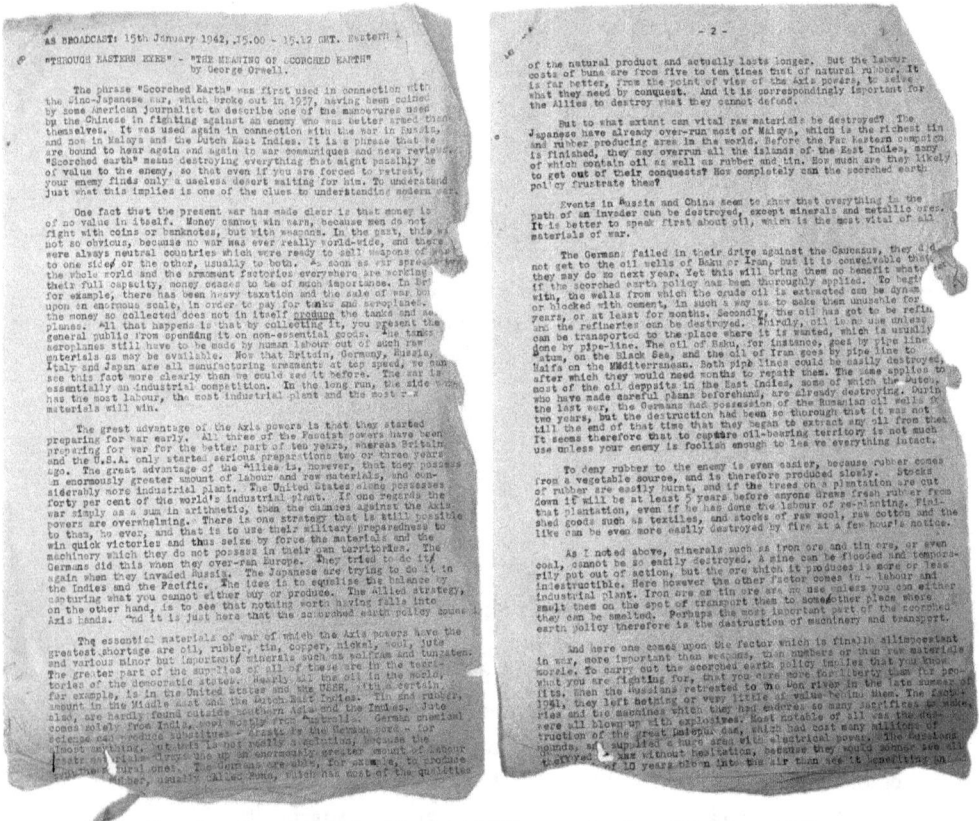

'The Meaning of Scorched Earth', BBC Eastern Service, 15 January 1942
(courtesy of the National Archives, New Delhi)

Life for Londoners like Orwell, living in the ruins of a city that had been blitzed by the Luftwaffe, was austere when 'The Meaning of Scorched Earth' was broadcast. The German U-boats were menacing British convoys, the war in the North African desert was going poorly, the Germans were approaching Moscow and the number of loved ones lost on land, sea and air was mounting. There must have been some resurgence of hope that fascism would be defeated considering the Americans had finally entered the war after the Japanese attack on Pearl Harbor.

Despite this cause for optimism, most must have realised it was going to be a long war and that the destruction wrought, in such a catastrophic and all-encompassing conflict, would make the peace a difficult one for citizens, especially those who had been displaced. The rationing and scarcity, so omnipresent in the bleak, war-ravaged world of Orwell's *Nineteen Eighty-Four* (1949) was to be an ongoing, grim reality for countless millions across Europe and Asia on the cessation of hostilities.

The phrase "Scorched Earth" was first used in connection with the Sino-Japanese war, which broke out in 1937, having been coined by some American journalist to describe one of the manoeuvres used by the Chinese in fighting against an enemy who was better armed than themselves. It was used again in connection with the war in Russia, and now in Malaya and the Dutch East Indies. It is a phrase we are bound to hear again and again in war communiques and news reviews. "Scorched earth" means destroying everything that might possibly be of value to the enemy, so that even if you are forced to retreat, your enemy finds only a useless desert waiting for him. To understand just what this implies is one of the clues to understanding modern war.

One fact that the present war has made clear is that money is of no value in itself. Money cannot win wars, because men do not fight with coins or banknotes, but with weapons. In the past, this was not so obvious, because no war was ever really world-wide, and there were always neutral countries which were ready to sell weapons of war to one side or the other, usually to both. As soon as war spread to the whole world and the armament factories everywhere are working to their full capacity, money ceases to be of much importance. In Britain for example, there has been heavy taxation and the sale of war bonds upon an enormous scale, in order to pay for the tanks and aeroplanes. [illegible] the money so collected does not in itself produce the tanks and aeroplanes. All that happens is by collecting it, you present (sic) the general public from spending it on non-essential goods. The tanks [illegible] aeroplanes still have to be made by human labour out of such raw materials as may be available. Now that Britain, Germany, Russia, Italy and Japan are all manufacturing armaments at top speed, we can see this fact more clearly than we could see it before. The war is essentially an industrial competition. In the long run, the side which has the most labour, the most industrial plant and the most raw materials will win.

The great advantage of the Axis powers is that they have started preparing for war early. All three of the Fascist powers have been preparing for war for the better part of ten years, whereas Britain and the U.S.A. only started serious preparations two or three years ago. The great advantage of the Allies is, however, that they possess an enormously greater amount of labour and raw materials, and considerably more industrial plant. The United States alone possesses forty percent of the world's industrial plant. If one regards the war simply as a sum in arithmetic, then the chances against the Axis powers are overwhelming. There is one strategy which is still possible to them, however, and that is to use their military preparedness to win quick victories and thus seize by force the materials and the machinery which they do not possess in their own territories. The Germans did this when they over-ran Europe. They tried to do it again when they invaded Russia. The Japanese are trying to do it in the Indies and the Pacific. The idea is to equalise the balance by capturing what you cannot either buy or produce. The Allied strategy, on the other hand, is to see that nothing worth having falls into Axis hands. And it is just here that the scorched earth policy comes in.

The essential materials of war of which the Axis powers have the greatest shortage are oil, rubber, tin, copper, nickel, wool, jute and various minor but important minerals such as wolfram and tungsten. The greater part of the supplies of all of these are in the territories of the democratic states. Nearly all the oil in the world, for example, is in the United States and the USSR, with a certain amount in the Middle East and the Dutch East Indies. Tin and rubber, also, are hardly found outside southern Asia and the Indies. Jute comes solely from India, wool mostly from Australia. German chemical science can produce substitutes - ersatz is the German word - for almost anything, but this is not really a solution, because the ersatz materials always use up an enormously greater amount of labour than the natural ones. The Germans are able, for example, to produce synthetic rubber, usually called Buna, which has most of the qualities of the natural product and actually lasts longer. But the labour costs of buna are from five to ten times that of natural rubber. It is far better, from the point of view of the Axis powers, to seize what they need by conquest. And it is correspondingly important for the Allies to destroy what they cannot defend.

'The Meaning of Scorched Earth', BBC Eastern Service, 15 January 1942

PAPER

> But to what extent can vital raw materials be destroyed? The Japanese have already over-run most of Malaya, which is the richest tin and rubber producing area in the world. Before the Far Eastern campaign is finished, they may overrun all the islands of the East Indies, many of which contain oil as well as rubber and tin. How much are they likely to get out of their conquests? How completely can the scorched earth policy frustrate them?
>
> Events in Russia and China seem to show that everything in the path of an invader can be destroyed, except minerals and metallic ores. It is better to speak first about oil, which is the most vital of all materials of war.
>
> The Germans failed in their drive against the Caucasus, they did not get to the oil wells of Baku or Iran, but it is conceivable that they may do so next year. Yet this will bring them no benefit whatever if the scorched earth policy has been thoroughly applied. To begin with, the wells from which the crude oil is extracted can be dynamited or blocked with cement, in such a way as to make them unusable for years, or at least for months. Secondly, the oil has got to be refined and the refineries can be destroyed. Thirdly, oil is no use unless it can be transported to the place where [illegible] is wanted, which is usually done by pipe-line. The oil of Baku, for instance, goes by pipe line [illegible] atum (sic), on the Black Sea, and the oil of Iran goes by pipe line to Haifa on the Mediterranean. Both pipe lines could be easily destroyed, after which they would need months to repair them. The same applies to most of the oil deposits in the East Indies, some of which the Dutch, who have made careful plans beforehand, are already destroying. During the last war, the Germans had possession of the Rumanian oil wells for two years, but the destruction had been so thorough that it was not till the end of that time that they began to extract any oil from them. It seems therefore that to capture oil-bearing territory is not much use unless your enemy is foolish enough to leave everything intact.
>
> To deny rubber to the enemy is even easier, because rubber comes from a vegetable source, and it is therefore produced slowly. Stocks of rubber are easily burnt, and if the trees on a plantation are cut down it will be at least five years before anyone draws fresh rubber from that plantation, even if he has done the labour of re-planting. Finished goods such as textiles, and stocks of raw wool, raw cotton and the like can be even more easily destroyed by fire at a few hour's (sic) notice.
>
> As I noted above, minerals such as iron ore and tin ore, or even coal, cannot be so easily destroyed. A mine can be flooded and temporarily put out of action, but the ore which it produces is more or less indestructible. Here however the other factor comes in – labour and industrial plant. Iron ore or tin ore are no use unless you can either smelt them on the spot or transport them to some other place where they can be smelted. Perhaps the most important part of the scorched earth policy therefore is the destruction of machinery and transport.
>
> And here one comes upon the factor which is finally all important in war, more important than weapons, than numbers or than raw materials morale (sic). To carry out the scorched earth policy implies that you know what you are fighting for, that you care more for liberty than for profits. When the Russians retreated to the Don river in the late summer of 1941, they left nothing or very little of value behind them. The factories and the machines which they had endures (sic) so many sacrifices to make, were all blown up with explosives. Most notable of all was the destruction of the great Dnieper dam, which had cost many millions of pounds, and supplied a huge area with electrical power. The Russians destroyed without hesitation, because they would sooner see all their work of 10 years blown into the air than seeing it benefitting TRUNCATES

'The Meaning of Scorched Earth', BBC Eastern Service, 15 January 1942. Transcript by Darcy Moore.

In the month after the broadcast, the impregnable British naval base at Singapore fell to the Japanese and the Battle for Australia commenced. Few would have guessed the absolute horror that was to unfold before the war finally concluded. There was the psychological terror of V-1 flying bombs for Londoners and the catastrophic loss of life in the fire-bombing of Dresden for the Germans. Orwell, serving as a war correspondent on the Continent for David Astor's *Observer* during the last days of the conflict, would see the death camps before the newsreels publicly screened the shocking enormity of Hitler's 'Final Solution'. A terrifying new weapon of mass annihilation, chillingly demonstrated during

August 1945 on the civilians of Hiroshima and Nagasaki, marked the beginning of a new epoch in human history.

Orwell was certainly not immune from the psychological impact of these horrors on his sense of optimism about what the future might hold. His mother died in 1943 and wife in 1945. Orwell now had the responsibility of raising an adopted son in a world where 'the atom bombs are piling up in the factories' (Orwell 1998 [1946]: 240). The bleak outlook that pervades *Nineteen Eighty-Four* is very understandable, even without factoring in the impact of Orwell's own worsening tubercular illness.

One line in the transcript stands out as an embodiment of Orwell's strange ability to write with completely convincing authority, something which, when pulled apart logically is somewhat dubious:

> To carry out the scorched earth policy implies that you know what you are fighting for, that you care more for liberty than for profits.

Orwell's analysis in mid-January 1942 – that any nation implementing a scorched earth policy had a genuine commitment to 'liberty' over 'profits' – was not a belief he was able to sustain while drafting *Nineteen Eighty-Four* in the years following the Second World War. The fight against German fascism had been won but the creeping threat of totalitarianism and the mind-boggling scope of the destruction during the last few years would not permit any rational acceptance that a scorched earth policy was any longer about liberty.

It is worth reflecting on the evolution of Orwell's thinking in the years after this radio broadcast. The experience of broadcasting wartime propaganda – although he felt he made it 'slightly less disgusting than it might otherwise have been' – significantly influenced his last novel, *Nineteen Eighty-Four* (Orwell 1998 [1942-1943]: 214). It is not hard to imagine Winston Smith, the protagonist, writing in his diary an analysis of Oceania's scorched earth policy during the unending wars with Eurasia or Eastasia. The development of Orwell's thinking on this matter is discernible in Emmanuel Goldstein's *The Theory and Practice of Oligarchical Collectivism*, the political tract within the novel which purports to analyse the function of war in that totalitarian state:

> The essential act of war is destruction, not necessarily of human lives, but of the products of human labour. War is a way of shattering to pieces, or pouring into the stratosphere, or sinking in the depths of the sea, materials which might otherwise be used to make the masses too comfortable, and hence, in the long run, too intelligent (Orwell 1997 [1949]: 198-199).

DARCY MOORE

Orwell, the writer, ultimately placed his faith in the primacy of language, not weapons or planned destruction, for fighting totalitarianism and ensuring liberty. This is evident throughout his major post-war essays and in the appendix, *The Principles of Newspeak*, which concludes his final novel. Orwell's cumulative political message was to resist organised impingement on the individual's liberty by any group – religious, political or artistic – who believed in 'concealing or preventing thought' (Orwell 1998 [1945]: 430).

MULK RAJ ANAND AND BALRAJ SAHNI

> Mr. Anand is one of the small group of Indian writers who prefers to write in English, and whose appearance during the past twenty years marks an important turning-point in Anglo-Indian relations (Orwell 1998 [1945]: 242).

There was a second transcript in Anand's private papers at this same archive; one that had not been lost. 'The Meaning of Sabotage' (Orwell 1942b) had originally been broadcast on 29 January 1942. It was also mentioned in Orwell's letter to Anand (Orwell 1998 [1941-1942]: 142-143). No other BBC transcripts could be located amongst his papers (although there may be more) which appears to confirm my theory that these are the transcripts mailed by Orwell. This talk was also read by Balraj Sahni (and had been censored by R. C. Hardman). The transcript was not annotated in Orwell's hand at the head of the first page with 'As broadcast. 10 mins 10 secs' like the copy Davison mentions in *CWGO* – but is the same text (ibid: 142).

The personal and professional relationship Orwell (the Anglo-Indian) had with Mulk Raj Anand and Balraj Sahni are contextually significant and worthy of further consideration (especially with Gandhi in mind). Anand, born in the Punjabi city of Peshawar, had his talent nurtured in England. He first visited London courtesy of a scholarship awarded on the silver wedding anniversary of George V and Queen Mary in the 1920s (Open University). During these four years he embraced left wing politics and the Indian independence movement (ibid). He joined a Marxist study group conducted by a trade union and was to become a lifelong socialist (ibid). He was a successful student and this first experience of England culminated in the award of a Doctorate in Philosophy from University College London (*ODNB* 2011). Anand returned to India in 1929 and cleaned latrines for three weeks at Gandhi's ashram in Ahmedabad (ibid). He was criticised by Gandhi for his Anglicised clothing and appearance (ibid). Anand also had the opportunity to attend a session of the Indian National Congress held in Lahore (ibid).

On returning to England, he was befriended by Virginia and Leonard Woolf who organised employment for the young writer at their Hogarth Press. T. S. Eliot published Anand's work in *The Criterion* and he had the opportunity to rub shoulders with many of the literary luminaries of his age, including D. H. Lawrence, W. B. Yeats and George Bernard Shaw (*ODNB* 2011). E. M. Forster was Anand's most influential early advocate, assisting with the publication of his first novel, *Untouchable* (1935) which had reputedly been rejected nineteen times by publishers (ibid). Anand's obituarists recount an anecdote about Gandhi providing feedback on an early draft of the novel which led to the writer making significant changes:

> Your untouchables sound too much like Bloomsbury intellectuals. You know an untouchable boy wouldn't talk in those long sentences (*Telegraph* 2004).

Forster provided significant support by writing a preface.

Orwell was another strong advocate. He recruited Anand to work at the BBC on a range of programmes that were never likely to find much of an audience. He suggested the title for Anand's 1942 novel, *The Sword and the Sickle*, and reviewed it positively. Orwell also wrote to the *Times Literary Supplement* objecting to unfair reviews of Anand's work (Orwell 1998 [1941-1942]: 337).

Douglas Kerr has pointed out that 'Anand was an anti-imperialist, a socialist, and an Indian nationalist. This was tricky for Orwell, who was highly suspicious of nationalism. But he defended Anand from charges of being anti-British and unfriendly to Anglo-Indians in his writing' (Kerr 2022: 165). Orwell always recognised Anand's literary importance but a note in his wartime diary (3 April 1942) clearly indicates why he was such an advocate during the early years of the war against Hitler. Orwell appreciated that this ardent Indian nationalist was 'genuinely anti-Fascist, and has done violence to his feelings, and probably to his reputation, by backing Britain up because he recognises that Britain is objectively on the anti-Fascist side' (Orwell 1998 [1941-1942]: 259). Orwell was in a similar situation himself. Eric Blair, who broadcast by agreement with the BBC under his pseudonym George Orwell, was conscious of potential damage to his own credibility. Ethically, he felt that defeating Hitler was more important than pursuing 'one's own revolution' (Orwell 1998 [1942-1943]: 214). Orwell knew he was being 'used by the British governing class' to broadcast propaganda to India and wrote to a friend explaining his position that 'one can't effectively remain outside the war & by working inside an institution like the BBC one can perhaps deodorise it to some small extent' (ibid).

DARCY MOORE

Balraj Sahni (1913-1973) was already working as an Indian programme assistant when Orwell joined the BBC in 1941. He had been educated at Harvard and knew Gandhi well, having lived with him for a year at an ashram during the late 1930s. This is where he met the Eton-educated Lionel Fielden (1896-1974), the director of All India Radio (AIR), in New Delhi. Fielden, whom Orwell detested (which is a fascinating tale but outside the scope of this piece) recruited Sahni in 1939 to join the BBC in London where he was soon broadcasting propaganda to Indian soldiers in Hindi (Fielden 1960: 228; Sahni 2017: 58-69).

Sahni's son and brother wrote biographies which emphasise Balraj's flamboyant non-conformity:

> He was unlike anyone else in the family. Influenced by the Romantic poets, he was a swash-buckling adventurer always looking for and taking on dangerous new challenges. He was a non-conformist and not one to pursue traditional lines of work … Dad was 'independent and impetuous by nature' and would 'do things that were off the beaten track'. 'Nothing risked, nothing gained' was his motto all his life (Sahni 2017: 35-36; Sahni 2019).

Orwell was very active in supporting his friend professionally. He introduced Sahni and his talented wife Damyanti (pronounced Dammo-ji) to Norman Marshall and organised for them to collaborate on 'Let's Act It Ourselves', a programme of discussions on dramatic presentation. Marshall, another non-conformist, was the owner of the Gate Theatre Studio, London, and a champion of what he called 'the non-commercial theatre' (Marshall 1948: 5). He developed expertise in avoiding the Lord Chamberlain's censorship rules by ensuring the audience were paid members of a theatre club (ibid: 12).

Orwell's personal and professional networks were extensive and not always in plain sight. It is possible that Orwell knew Marshall via his aunt, Nellie Limouzin. She was an actress and had been a significant source of information for her nephew's first professionally published article, about censorship in England, 'La Censure en Angleterre', in Henri Barbusse's *Monde*, in October 1928 (Moore 2020: 32).

Anand was later to have the melancholy task of telling Sahni that Orwell's wife, Eileen O'Shaughnessy, had died in late March 1945. Sahni wrote to Orwell fondly and compassionately:

> … you endeared yourselves to us greatly, through your work and your sincerity. This news has made us very sad indeed (Orwell 1998 [1945]: 390).

Sahni was to become an accomplished film actor and director in India. Principled and revered for his portrayals of the underprivileged, Sahni was a leading star during the Golden Age of Indian cinema. He also experienced the grief of losing his wife, who died unexpectedly in 1947.

Both Anand and Sahni were likely sources of up-to-date information about Gandhi. Peter Davison's speculations regarding the extent to which Sahni's knowledge of the Mahātmā influenced Orwell's writings on Gandhi, especially his important essay written in 1949, the year after the Indian's assassination, are worthy of further reflection (Orwell 2010: 521).

Sahni on a postage stamp of India (2013)

FUTURE DIRECTIONS

There appeared to be vast swathes of Mulk Raj Anand's literary estate left to catalogue in New Delhi. Anand had such a significant collaboration with Orwell at the BBC there could possibly be missing transcripts or letters to be discovered amongst these papers. A knee-deep pile of folders – marked 'photographs' – that I was not permitted to view needs further investigation. There may be images of the literary and BBC circles that Anand and Orwell shared. Shots, taken of Orwell during his BBC days, first appeared in the book, *Talking to India* (1943), which he edited. It is possible that there were other photos taken during that shoot which did not make the cut but could be in those folders.

Please feel encouraged to make contact if you are planning to pursue research in the National Archives of India in New Delhi (or the state archives in Lucknow, Patna or Kolkata) as there are many leads to pursue. I am more than happy to assist with areas worthy of further investigation. Who knows what treasures, hidden away in these and other archives, are yet to be found!

- Special thanks to the staff at the National Archives of India in New Delhi for their assistance. The late Peter Davison's research provided the information necessary to track down this lost transcript and to understand contextually Orwell's relationship with Balraj Sahni and Mulk Raj Anand. Thank you, as ever, to Peter Marks and Douglas Kerr for their insights. Both suggested that the illegible word in the transcript 'atum' is Batumi, a Georgian port on the Black Sea.
- An early version of this essay was published at my website: https://www.darcymoore.net/2024/01/19/lost-orwell-bbc-radio-transcript-found/

DARCY MOORE REFERENCES AND FURTHER READING

Anand, Mulk Raj (1940) *Untouchable*, London: Penguin

Bluemel, Kristin (2004) *George Orwell and the Radical Eccentrics: Intermodernism in Literary London*, London: Palgrave Macmillan

Brander, Laurence (1954) *George Orwell*, London: Longmans, Green & Co

Fielden, Lionel (1960) *The Natural Bent*, London: André Deutsch

Kerr, Douglas (2022) *Orwell & Empire*, Oxford: Oxford University Press

Marshall, Norman (1947) *The Other Theatre*, London: John Lehmann

Moore, Darcy (2020) Orwell's Aunt Nellie, *George Orwell Studies*, Vol. 4, No.2 pp 30-44

Moore, Darcy (2022) Orwell's rats, *George Orwell Studies*, Vol. 7, No.1 pp 92-101

Moore, Darcy (2023) Orwell's ayah, *Darcy Moore's Blog*, 24 January. https://www.darcymoore.net/2023/01/24/orwells-ayah/

Oxford Dictionary of National Biography (*ODNB*) (2011) Mulk Raj Anand (1905-2004) by Niven, Alastair

Open University (ND) *Making Britain: Mulk Raj Anand*. Available online at https://www5.open.ac.uk/research-projects/making-britain/content/mulk-raj-anand, accessed on 4 February 2024

Orwell, George (1940) *Down and Out in Paris and London*, London: Penguin

Orwell, George (2010) *George Orwell: A Life in Letters,* Davison, Peter (ed.) London: Harvill Secker

Orwell, George (1942a) The Meaning of Scorched Earth, BBC Eastern Service, 15 January (courtesy of the National Archives, New Delhi)

Orwell, George (1942b) The Meaning of Sabotage, BBC Eastern Service, 29 January (courtesy of the National Archives, New Delhi)

Orwell, George (1943) *Talking to India; A Selection of English Language Broadcasts to India*, London: George Allen & Unwin Ltd

Orwell, George (1997) *Nineteen Eighty-Four, The Complete Works of George Orwell, Vol. IX*, Davison, Peter (ed.) London: Secker & Warburg

Orwell, George (1998 [1941-1942]) *All Propaganda Is Lies: 1941-1942, The Complete Works of George Orwell, Vol. XIII*, Davison, Peter (ed.) London: Secker & Warburg

Orwell, George (1998 [1942-1943]) *Keeping Our Little Corner Clean: 1942-1943, The Complete Works of George Orwell, Vol. XIV*, Davison, Peter (ed.) London: Secker & Warburg

Orwell, George (1998 [1945]) *I Belong to the Left: 1945, The Complete Works of George Orwell, Vol. XVII*, Davison, Peter (ed.) London: Secker & Warburg

Orwell, George (1998 [1946]) *Smothered Under Journalism: The Complete Works of George Orwell, Vol. XVIII*, Davison, Peter (ed.) London: Secker & Warburg

Orwell, George (1998 [1947-1948]) *It Is What I Think: The Complete Works of George Orwell, Vol. XIX*, Davison, Peter (ed.) London: Secker & Warburg

Sahni, Balraj (1979) *Balraj Sahni: An Autobiography*, Hind Pocket Books

Sahni, Bhisham (2017) *Balraj Sahni: My Brother*, New Delhi: National Book Trust

Sahni, Parikshat (2019) *The Non-Conformist: Memories of My Father Balraj Sahni*, New Delhi: Penguin Random House India

Telegraph (2004) Obituary: Mulk Raj Anand, 29 September. Available online at https://www.telegraph.co.uk/news/obituaries/1472853/Mulk-Raj-Anand.html, accessed on 4 February 2024

West, W.J. (1985a) *Orwell: The War Broadcasts*, London: Duckworth & Co/BBC Books

West, W.J. (1985b) *Orwell: The War Commentaries*, London: Duckworth & Co/ BBC Books

West, W.J. (1992) *The Larger Evils:* Nineteen Eighty-Four*, the Truth Behind the Satire*, Edinburgh: Canongate Press

Zivin, Joselyn (1999) 'Bent': A colonial subversive and Indian Broadcasting, *Past & Present*, No. 162 pp 195-220

NOTE ON THE CONTRIBUTOR

Darcy Moore is a deputy principal at a secondary school in New South Wales. He blogs at *darcymoore.net* and his Twitter handle is @Darcy1968. His Orwell Studies Library can be accessed at darcymoore.net/orwell-collection/. He can be contacted by email: dfjmoore@gmail.com.

PAPER

ARTICLE

Eileen, '1984' and *Nineteen Eighty-Four*

Did a poem by George Orwell's first wife, Eileen O'Shaughnessy Blair, influence his choices – of the title and even the themes and imagery – in Nineteen Eighty-Four? *John Rodden examines the contentions and weighs the evidence.*

TO CATCH A THIEF? PLAGIARISM AND ORWELL AT 70

Readers of George Orwell should be forgiven for failing to realise that we are now approaching an anniversary that resonates with special force today in light of a swirl of controversies about Orwell's moral standards and literary integrity: the seventieth anniversary – Christmas 1954 – of the opening round of plagiarism charges against him.

Within three weeks of the two BBC 'teleplays' broadcast on 12 and 16 December 1954 – BBC small screen adaptations which caused a national sensation in the UK and political controversies that lasted months – influential Marxist and radical critics of Orwell charged him with plagiarising *1984* (they always preferred the numerical title) from Yevgeni Zamyatin's anti-utopia, *We*. Elsewhere, I have discussed why these Orwell critics waited more than five years since the novel's publication date (June 1949).[1]

So I will not review that topic here, except to note that an avalanche of allegations followed in the next seven decades and continue to our day. These accusations range from reiterations of the original indictments about his thefts from Zamyatin, which were advanced by Isaac Deutscher and R. Palme Dutt in January 1955[2] – to waves of subsequent claims involving at least three dozen other works of fiction and nonfiction. Within two years, those accusations had received respectful treatment across the Atlantic – from George Woodcock and Irving Howe, among others – in the pages of the *New Republic,* various literary quarterlies, and other liberal American and Canadian publications.[3]

Not today: suffice it to say that these particular charges have carried little or no weight in the twenty-first century with serious scholars. I address in detail this history of these and other plagiarism charges against him in a forthcoming study, *George Orwell: Plagiarist and Predator?* Here I pursue a more immediate issue of 'influence' that is easily conflated with 'sources', 'parallels' and 'plagiarisms', none of which Orwell's accusers take the pains to define or distinguish – including critics such as Deutscher and Daphne Patai (in *The Orwell Mystique: A Study in Male Ideology*, 1984).

The newest charge of unacknowledged 'influence' treated as a form of 'plagiarism', which has received widespread publicity since the summer of 2023, is the contention that Orwell's choice of the year 1984 for the title of his last novel owes to his wife, Eileen O'Shaughnessy Blair. That charge was first published in 1999, when a poem of Eileen came to public notice. Sally Coniam, formerly on the staff of Eileen's alma mater, Sunderland Church High School, came across the poem in the 1934 school magazine. Her 1999 *TLS* article included a reprint and analysis of the poem. She suggested that not only the title date but also the anti-utopian themes, imagery and leitmotifs of *Nineteen Eighty-Four* derived from the poem. The *TLS* title – 'Orwell and the origins of *Nineteen Eighty-Four*' – lent weight to the view that Eileen's poem inspired Orwell's novel.[4]

Despite the 1999 *TLS* article, as well as mentions of Eileen's poem by subsequent scholars, the idea that it may have inspired the title and even content of Orwell's novel – and that both Orwell and the scholarly community deviously omitted reference to his debts to her – has only gained broad circulation as a result of Anna Funder's best-selling *Wifedom: Mrs Orwell's Invisible Life* (2023). Or rather, to the headline-grabbing international reception of her biography of Orwell. That reception has furnished Orwell's long-time critics on the left a new angle on the history of his alleged plagiarisms in *Nineteen Eighty-Four*.

Grieving that Eileen's 'brilliance' had so long gone unheralded, *The Times* of London deplored that Orwell 'stole her ideas'.[5] As a *Brisbane Times* contributor wrote:

> As George is piss-farting around in the hills of Catalonia, playing at being a soldier, Eileen is working in the nerve centre of the resistance. … It is Eileen who keeps the couple solvent. Eileen who brings home tales of censorship from her wartime job at the Ministry of Information. Eileen who first writes a dystopian work called 'End of the Century, 1984'. *Wifedom* is a damning catalogue of the ways women are diminished, ignored, trivialised and banished to the footnotes.[6]

For the first time, mainstream publications gave extensive attention to the 'Orwell the plagiarist' allegations (what could be worse than 'credit snatching' from your own wife?! asked one reviewer). 'Plagiarism begins at home,' wrote another.[7] Denunciations of Orwell's perfidy filled the pages of leading newspapers and magazines throughout the English-speaking world.

My focus in this essay is on the plagiarism allegations pertaining to *Nineteen Eighty-Four*. We should note here, however, that critics'

JOHN RODDEN   allegations about Orwell's thefts did not start with *Nineteen Eighty-Four*. As if he were Napoleon in *Animal Farm* – who steals Snowball's idea to build the windmill and then presents Snowball's windmill design in a barnyard meeting as his own – Orwell is also accused of having put his name to Eileen's idea to pen a Stalinist critique in the form of a fable. A *Guardian* writer posed the rhetorical question: 'Was Mrs Orwell the real genius behind *Animal Farm*?' The *Sydney Morning Herald* reviewer answered the question by formally acknowledging Eileen's co-author credit forthwith, casually discussing the fable's impact on Cold War geopolitics as follows: 'Fiction has always served large truths. Orwell and O'Shaughnessy used it to devastating effect in *Animal Farm* to arraign Stalinism.'[8]

THE POET AND THE PINCHER?

Despite their confidently voiced vilifications of Orwell and his (male) biographers as co-conspirators in the patriarchal world of Orwell scholars – who have colluded with him in a 'theft-and-erasure' scheme[9] – I suspect that Anna Funder and her reviewers know little or nothing about the previous history of dispute about Orwell's 'plagiarisms' in *Nineteen Eighty-Four*. Nor would they especially care. The focus of *Wifedom* and the reviews is not literary but biographical, not about the nature of Orwell's debts to other fictions but rather about his 'theft' or failure to 'credit' Eileen's contribution to *Nineteen Eighty-Four*.

As I have noted, similar allegations have been advanced in *Wifedom* and elsewhere about Orwell's 'theft' from Eileen regarding *Animal Farm*. Of course, given that Eileen died more than four years before the novel's appearance, assertions about her 'contribution' to *Nineteen Eighty-Four* cannot be advanced in the same terms as in the case of *Animal Farm*, written in the form of a fable, thanks to Eileen's advice, contend some critics. In the case of *NE-F*'s composition, there are no third-hand remarks to report, as prevails with *Animal Farm* and colleagues' remarks about its style and sensibility; a few friends of Eileen or George made observations that *Animal Farm* possessed a gaiety, a lightness of spirit, or a whimsy that represents a departure from his earlier work.[10] A biographical approach that involves interaction between Eileen and George is not, therefore, possible regarding the development of *Nineteen Eighty-Four*. Instead, Funder and the reviewers seize on Eileen's 1934 poem in *The Chronicle*, an alma mater publication of Sunderland Church High School, which was titled '1984 – End of the Century'. They would have us believe that Orwell took the title for his dystopia from Eileen's poem, and that its predictions about the year 1984 at the century's 'end' inspired Orwell's dystopian meditations, predictably far grimmer given what his brother-in-law Humphrey Dakin once termed his 'gloomy George' temperament.

Downplayed if not ignored or omitted – probably from sheer ignorance by some accusers – is any discussion of why Eileen herself chose the year 1984 for part of the title of her poem. The title arose from the projected anniversary of Sunderland Church High School a half-century ahead. That is to say, the year 1934 witnessed the school celebrating its fiftieth anniversary; the school magazine's editors proposed that Eileen contribute something to the anniversary issue. Eileen chose to look ahead to the school's projected centenary date: hence the choice of the title. The poem has nothing to do with any dire vision of the late twentieth century, nothing to do with any fateful meaning ascribed by Orwell to the year '1984'. (Eileen published the poem in June 1934, a year before meeting Eric Blair. Did he read it? Despite all the allegations about his 'theft' and failed 'acknowledgement', no evidence has surfaced that he ever knew about it, let alone remembered it many years later.)

Those facts have not impeded accusers from alleging – even in the pages of The Orwell Society's official publication – that Orwell 'cancelled' Eileen's contribution to the title, themes and vision of *Nineteen Eighty-Four*. In The Orwell Society *Journal*, Ann Kronbergs' review ('Eileen: Hidden from history', Autumn 2023) of *Wifedom* devotes substantial attention to claims that Eileen's 1934 poem influenced the language and imagery of *Nineteen Eighty-Four*. Kronbergs follows earlier contentions by two *TLS* reviewers, among others, who support this view. She speaks appreciatively that a 2023 *TLS* reviewer of *Wifedom* (Eileen M. Hunt) 'flags up how Orwell switched the original title of his novel from *Last Man in Europe* [sic] to *Nineteen Eighty-Four* without acknowledging his first wife's poem anywhere in his text'. Kronbergs says that Eileen's poem was 'a likely source' for *Nineteen Eighty-Four* and quotes approvingly Hunt's claim that all the 'findings' supporting this contention are 'either ignored … or dismissed as coincidence' by 'most of Orwell's leading biographers and scholars. According to Hunt, this deliberate suppression of Eileen's contribution to *Nineteen Eighty-Four* – committed first by her own husband and then by Orwell biographers and scholars – is due to 'the patriarchal biases of Orwell studies'.

There are a number of problems with these contentions. First, we do not know if the 'original title' of *Nineteen Eighty-Four* was *Last Man in Europe*. I believe that it may not have been the first working title of his novel. The facsimile publication of the surviving 381-page manuscript of *Nineteen Eighty-Four*, edited by Peter Davison – which amounts to roughly 40 per cent of the book – was published in 1984, including a preface by the manuscript's owner, Daniel G. Siegel.[11] As notations in the manuscript make clear, Orwell

ARTICLE

JOHN RODDEN considered at least two other dates for the setting (1980 and 1982) before adopting the working title of *The Last Man in Europe*, and subsequently *Nineteen Eighty-Four*.

Do the 'findings' about Eileen's poem take into account the earlier dates for the setting of '1980' and '1982'? Evidently not. Likewise, ignored or omitted – perhaps from sheer ignorance – is any acknowledgement in *Wifedom* about these dates in the manuscript version[12].

Nobody has 'dismissed as coincidence' the concurrence between the title year of Eileen's poem. All this reflects a fundamental misunderstanding of the distinctions between literary parallels, resonances and sources. The title and content of Eileen's poem are not in any sense a 'likely source' for *Nineteen Eighty-Four*. Nor can Eileen's line about 'Telepathic Station 9' be said to 'herald the telescreens in the world of Winston Smith'. Such echoes represent parallels and resonances: both Eileen and Orwell were fascinated by the utopian visions of H.G. Wells and had read Huxley's *Brave New World*. The vision and language of Eileen's were part of the cultural *zeitgeist* of the 1930s and 1940s.

Beyond all this, if indeed George Orwell did eventually settle on his title date as a gesture to Eileen, one should ask: who authorised literary critics to rule that husbands and wives are obligated to acknowledge publicly a gesture of personal sentiment? Since when has the job description of literary critic been revised into 'self-acknowledged legislator of the world'? Who at the Ministry of Truth certifies literary scholars to become Behavioral Police agents? The entire discussion of the marital relationship between George and Eileen is mired in legalistic argument, self-righteous moralism and prurient, sanctimonious meddlesomeness.[13]

If we may dare to ask these critics to deign to address a practical matter: how is a novelist supposed to go about 'acknowledging his first wife's poem anywhere in his text'? Here again, novelists are not scholars. A novel is not a scholarly work that includes citations and footnotes.[14] Some scholars – I am among them – believe that Orwell's choice to have Winston Smith open his diary entries on 4 April ('Down with Big Brother!' he writes defiantly) represented his veiled *hommage* to Eileen, whose funeral date was 3 April, and that he began his novel with this memory and intention firmly in mind. Yet, of course, this possibility is nowhere explicitly 'acknowledged in his text'.

IGNORANCE IS STRENGTH!

Nor should readers accept the blithe and moralistic assertion that Eileen has been 'cancelled' by scholars of Orwell, as *Wifedom* proclaims. Only the negligence of a 'biographer' to consult the history of Orwell scholarship and the ideologically motivated ignorance of reviewers to accept her 'biography' as gospel can account for contentions that Eileen is 'invisible'.

Yes, of course, she *will* seem 'invisible' if reviewers limit their reading to *Wifedom* and swallow its contentions without verifying them. Or if the author herself does not acknowledge what other biographers have had to say about Eileen, even long before Sylvia Topp's *Eileen: The Making of George Orwell* (2020). Anna Funder is so busy inventing pages and pages of chapter-length scenes that she terms 'fictions of inclusion' – fantasised scenarios complete with invented dialogues and an omniscient narrator's reports of the characters' thoughts (and thoughtcrimes) – that she is blind to the extensive attention Orwell's 'male biographers' have devoted to Eileen. They are simply accused of having 'cancelled' Eileen through their 'fictions of omission' – which *Wifedom* purportedly must redress.

Eileen Blair has never been 'hidden from history' by earlier biographers. For more than 45 years, she has been prominently honoured and written about with respect and affection. Peter Stansky and William Abrahams, in *The Transformation* (1979), include a 70-page chapter titled 'Eileen', one of the book's four chapters. Jeffrey Meyers, in *Orwell: Wintry Conscience of a Generation* (2000), also devotes her a section, 'Eileen and Wigan Pier 1935-37'. Likewise, Orwell's other biographers give her substantial treatment, with dozens of references – more citations, in every single case, than any other person aside from George Orwell himself.

Indeed, I regret to inform readers that *Wifedom* is not 'a monumental work that almost defies description', not 'a tour de force' distinguished by 'extraordinary research' – whatever notions uninformed reviewers may harbour about the author 'poring over books, documents, letters, government files' etc. etc. Nor is it a 'spectacular achievement of scholarship' written 'with the precision of a historian'.[15] Perhaps others beside myself will doubt too, if they have read the impressive and careful scholarship conducted by Orwell's biographers (and by Sylvia Topp in *Eileen*), that 'there is exhilaration in reading every brilliant word'.[16] Finally, having devoted a substantial sum of my own intellectual energies to George Orwell's afterlife and heritage, I do not find – my esteem for the author's polemical skills notwithstanding – that 'Funder is the perfect writer to integrate Orwell's legacy.'[17]

Let us return, however, to the matter immediately at hand: Eileen, her poem and Orwell's novel. *Wifedom* quotes Eileen's poem in full, mentioning none of the above, noting only that 'it is possible that Orwell's title … is a homage to it'. Yes, that is possible. No problem. Then she goes much further with her implication:

JOHN RODDEN

I imagine them discussing literature, especially poetry. ... He'd set out initially to be a poet; her favorite writers were the Lake Poets. She might have mentioned a poem she'd written the year before, projecting a future of telepathy and mind control in 1984.[18]

That summary – 'a future of telepathy and mind control' – is an absurd distortion of both the contents and originality of the poem, based solely on passing references to a 'Telepathic Station 9' and 'manana-minded ten-year-olds'. The latter phrase also likely owed to her recent reading of *Brave New World* (1932). Equally likely is that Orwell 'might have mentioned' (as *Wifedom* phrases so many judgements that it delivers in the absence of evidence) that one of his Eton teachers had been Huxley. Probably Eileen and George discussed *Brave New World* and the work of H.G. Wells during that spring of 1935. (Wells was a boyhood hero of Eric Blair; Eileen was also likely familiar with Wells's utopias and scientific romances, possibly even before her Oxford days.)[19] The resonance of her poem with any motifs in *Nineteen Eighty-Four* more plausibly owes to these shared enthusiasms.

Advocates for a case that Orwell committed the dastardly act of pinching the idea for his novel's title (and more) from Eileen advance their claims in apparent ignorance of all this. Far worse, however, is the ignorance about how absorbed with dates Orwell became as he worked on his novel. Many readers know that his working title for months was *The Last Man in Europe* because he wrote a letter to his publisher in which he used that title. The letter was published in the four-volume *The Collected Essays, Journalism and Letters of George Orwell* (*CEJL*), published in 1968 and edited by Sonia Orwell and Ian Angus.

As I noted earlier, what is less well known, though easily available these days to anyone who bothers to inspect the surviving manuscript of the novel – a facsimile of which was published four decades ago – is that Orwell set the novel in 1980, then 1982, before settling finally on 1984. This revelation was not hidden away; it was treated as a major discovery, both in the Preface and Introduction to the facsimile edition.[20] Siegel writes in a prefatory statement about his excitement on learning, during a visit to New York in May 1969, that a manuscript of the novel existed. Inspecting the manuscript, his attention was immediately drawn to the dates, both of them crossed out as Orwell's revisions proceeded; he was so astonished that he hesitated to purchase the manuscript, briefly doubting its authenticity.

At first, I was not absolutely convinced I really was looking at *Nineteen Eighty-Four*. ... [O]ne of the first leaves I examined contained the date 1980, and later I spotted 1982. This was not reassuring. ... What could be the basis for 1980 or 1982? As I continued to turn pages, the history of Winston Smith came to life. ... In an instant I knew I was going to filter a great anti-utopian manuscript from the memory hole... (p. vi).

Peter Davison, the facsimile version's editor, then drew attention in the Introduction to specifics, particularly the 'intriguing' alteration of the dates throughout the manuscript. Compared with the final manuscript, he noted, the earlier versions feature several interesting differences.

> The most intriguing is undoubtedly the date 1984. It is obvious from the original that the future was to be set in 1980, Winston's diary beginning on April 4th of that year. The year was then changed to 1982 in ink and 1982 was what was typed. ... Both were then changed to 1984. It would seem that it was some way through the process of revision, even of re-revision, that the date of 1984 was chosen (p. 23).

On three occasions in Part One of the novel, '1980' is typed, then amended to '1982' and then finally changed to '1984'. One of Orwell's most famous passages initially reads:

> A tremor had gone through his bowels. To mark the paper was the decisive act. Rather clumsily he wrote: April 4th, 1980 (p. 23).

Two later passages read:

> No sooner had he written the words than a sense of complete helplessness came upon him. To begin with, he did not know with any certainty that this *was* 1982.

> Suddenly he began writing in sheer panic, only imperfectly aware of what he was setting down. His small but childish handwriting straggled up and down the page, shedding first its capital letters, and finally even its full stops.

> April 4th 1982. Last night to the flicks ... (p. 9).

I believe that Orwell was much preoccupied with dates because he had apparently resolved that his hero, Winston Smith, would be just short of forty years old in the future. A key alteration, in order to accommodate '1982' was the following:

> Since he [Winston] was fairly sure that his age was 39, and he believed that he had been born in 1942 or 1943 but it was impossible nowadays to pin down any date within a year or two (p. 27).

In the final manuscript version, these birth dates were changed to '1944 or 45' in order to keep the same age span for the target year 1984. The shift to 1984 had the additional appeal of coinciding with the projected age of Orwell's son, Richard Blair, who was born

JOHN RODDEN in 1944 and would be 39 in April 1984. It seems likely that Orwell's rumination about dates as he proceeded to revise the manuscript in 1948 led him to swerve from his working title at that time, 'The Last Man in Europe', and to settle on a title featuring a date.

The manuscript does not make clear whether '1980' or '1982' served as earlier working title dates (no manuscript title page survives), but it seems quite possible that Orwell was veering between a title featuring his portrait of Winston as 'the last man' and a title that would encapsulate the idea of 'the future'. I suspect that his ongoing ruminations about dates provoked him to question 'The Last Man in Europe' as a title. Perhaps he recognised that there is no 'Europe' in the novel, for Winston does not live 'in Europe', and altering the title to 'The Last Man in Oceania' would have confused readers with the expectation that the novel was set in the far Pacific. Perhaps Orwell also realised the appeal of a date in order to underscore Winston's urge, voiced in his diary, to 'communicate with the future'. Revealingly, the manuscript originally read: 'It was not so easy to communicate with the future, 1982.' Then he changed the sentence to: 'with the future, 1984'. Ultimately, he altered it to the published sentence:

> But it was not so simple, this business of communicating with the future.

On this view, while the phrase 'the last man' remained important to Orwell – and represents a leitmotif in Part Three of the novel (the phrase is quoted by O'Brien during the torture scenes in the Ministry of Love) – Orwell's emergent conviction that his novel should serve as a cautionary warning issued by 'the future', as it were, apparently led him in a different direction. It persuaded him that a title date evoking his vision of a possible totalitarian future – now set in 1984 – represented the most direct and powerful title choice.

I have dwelt at length on Orwell's careful deliberations, and repeated revisions, of the setting's date, including extensive reference to the date, in Part One and Part Three (e.g., in the scenes set in Charrington's antique shop),[21] in order to suggest that the idea of a title date – whether '1980', '1982' or '1984' – was likely a consideration as the novel progressed.

To summarise: I believe that Orwell was mulling the idea of a title date throughout the later stages of composition and revision. His decision to settle on a date became ever more appealing when he pondered further that his futuristic nightmare was a world in which his son Richard might live, as if he were 39-year-old Winston Smith.

By contrast, as in the case of the 'fiction of inclusion' that Eileen 'co-authored' *Animal Farm*, the accusations that her sole publication

– a poem which appeared in the 1934 issue of the Sunderland Church High School for Girls' magazine and looked forward fifty years to the school's centenary – inspired the title and dystopian vision of *Nineteen Eighty-Four* is a conjecture without evidence to support it.[22] As we have seen, the claim ignores the fact that two dates for the setting of the novel in earlier drafts of it, which may have served as the possible titles before his announced working title to his publisher, *The Last Man in Europe*, were '1980' and '1982'. Virtually no biographer or scholar of Orwell – with the notable exception of Gordon Bowker – has taken such contentions about Eileen's poem seriously – with good reason.[23]

What is so regrettable, here and elsewhere in the feminist critique of Orwell, is how a valuable historical discovery – the existence of Eileen's poem and the resonance of a few lines with motifs in Orwell's novel – is accompanied by inflated claims that distort the significance and meaning of the discovery and thereby invite its casual dismissal, tempting readers to discount the value of the discovery altogether.[24] For instance, while most of Orwell's biographers did accurately determine that no historical evidence exists to link Eileen's poem with *Nineteen Eighty-Four*, they proceeded to conclude that the poem was not sufficiently relevant or significant to mention in a discussion of the novel. I regard that conclusion as a misjudgement: the 'coincidence' is so arresting that some acknowledgment of the poem was warranted.

Yet there is latitude for disagreement on the point without hurling accusations that male conspirators have 'cancelled' or 'diminished, ignored, trivialised and banished' Eileen. (Bowker may have gone too far in his vague statement that Eileen's poem furnished a possible 'explanation' for the choice of the year 1984; but he was certainly right to devote a paragraph to its existence.)

Likewise in the category of excessive claims for the poem: the contention that it served as a (or even 'the') 'likely source' for *Nineteen Eighty-Four*. No persuasive evidence has been adduced that it was a 'likely source' for Orwell's title, let alone for the imagery and themes, in the novel. A 'possible' source? For the title? Yes, I would not rule that out. Certainly it is 'possible' that a memory of the year 1984 in her poem's title converged with his own thinking in late 1948 and early 1949, as he was still mulling the final title and – if it did not motivate him, then at least gratified him to realise – that his choice of title would honour their 'marriage of true minds' – whatever its flaws and failings.

Remaining receptive to such possibilities, given the absence of any evidence whatsoever about 'sources' or 'influences' – preserves an open stance that invites further scholarly inquiry, which a vibrant scholarly community should encourage.

ARTICLE

JOHN RODDEN   SICKBED "FICTION OF INCLUSION"?

We need not castigate George in order to commend Eileen. We need not manufacture or distort evidence in order to render her visible – as scholars such as Sylvia Topp and Angela Smith have reminded us in recent years.

No evidence exists that Eileen's poem in the Sunderland Church High School magazine for 1934 influenced the conception of *Nineteen Eighty-Four*'s themes or its title. Nor is the poem ultimately 'dystopian' in any sense[25] – just the reverse, it is decidedly auspicious about the future circa 1984. The third and final stanza, titled 'The Phoenix', projects nothing less than a utopian future in which 'past and future may agree'. The speaker, as if enacting a version of St John's apocalyptic visions in the Book of Revelation, glimpses the rise of 'worlds [that] plume again their fairest feathers / And in their clearest songs may give / Welcome to all spontaneous weathers'.

Did Orwell ever read the poem? We do not know. No evidence has ever surfaced that he did so. I regard it as quite possible that he read it around 1935, soon after meeting Eileen.[26] Or might a copy have been among Eileen's personal effects in April 1945, when Orwell returned after her Newcastle funeral to close up their Wallington cottage? Again: it is possible. We do not know.

Did Orwell remember the poem when he was striving, furiously, desperately, almost fifteen years later to complete *Nineteen Eighty-Four*? Possibly so. Again, we do not know.

And yet: this much we do know. In any study of literary influence, the burden of proof rests with those who claim the influence, that is, a responsibility to provide supporting documentation about the claim itself as well as its scale and relevance. Outsized claims borne of exaggeration or mere assertion represent forms of distortion in their own right. Furthermore, responsible biographical and historical scholarship rests on evidence, not surmise or innuendo, let alone allegation.

Adherence to those standards is a special imperative when claims of literary influence become the foundation of grave accusations against a writer, particularly when they are advanced in terms of that potentially annihilating P-word: plagiarism.

THE PROPHECY AND THE RECKONING: WHITHER ORWELL?

In closing, may I ask the reader's indulgence? The words of a scholarly second self echo in my mind amid the current calls for Orwell's cancellation.

More than thirty-five years ago, I wrote: '[R]eaders, male and sometimes female, have treated Orwell's slighting remarks about women as beneath mention.' Addressing the existence in some circles of an 'Orwell cult', I added that, in part, 'the Orwell cult,' was a 'cult of masculinity'. The emergent feminist consciousness among intellectuals would 'probably play a large role in further reshaping [Orwell's] reputation, if not to some degree undermining it'.[27]

Contrary to its grandiose claims for *Wifedom*'s originality, recognition of Orwell's traditionalist attitudes and unprogressive treatment of Eileen and other women, abetted by (chiefly male) admirers, is nothing new. And whatever their excesses, the passion of Anna Funder and other recent feminist critics has partly arisen from their genuine admiration for aspects of his life and *oeuvre*. They are highly critical of Orwell because their early encounters with his work led them to expect far more from him. 'The gender gap is there,' I wrote, noting that 'the disappointment is keen', a consequence of 'the pain of seeking to identify with a figure, only to be deflected'.

> Their feeling of letdown, which their high expectations deepen and sharpen, points to the large problem of heroic identification across gender. ...[All this] reflects variously the urge for a heroism that transcends gender modeling, the longing for intellectual heroes who are heroines too, the acquiescence to gradual social change, and the recognition or evasion of the differences between present and past. ...The masculine voice of Orwell's prose, his association of moral courage with physical courage, his own 'manly' example that socialism is something to fight and die for, his railing against the 'softness' of 'machine civilization', his emphasis on 'hard' experience rather than theory. ... Orwell the man and writer projected a virile image especially attractive to male intellectuals. ... Indeed part of his appeal has always been his capacity to make intellectual life seem manly, not feminine, a calling of unusual adventure, larger than life. Male intellectuals have, therefore, projected their own dreams on to him...[28]

Today we are witnessing how the feminist consciousness of the twenty-first century is 'reshaping Orwell's reputation' anew. Where it will ultimately lead is still uncertain: if it be for good, further toward the undermining of 'the Orwell cult'; if it be for ill, toward the undermining of a long-valued and still-valuable intellectual legacy.

JOHN RODDEN

NOTES

[1] See my chapter, Orwell and the Marxists: The Hundred Years' Culture War? in *George Orwell: Plagiarist and Predator* (forthcoming)

[2] Deutscher was widely known and celebrated as the biographer of Stalin in June 1949, which was published in the same week as Orwell's *Nineteen Eighty-Four*. The first volume of his biography of Leon Trotsky appeared in the fall of 1954; Palme Dutt was the chief theoretician of the Communist Party of Great Britain for 40-odd years as editor of *Labour Monthly*. Deutscher's essay appeared in his widely read and admired collection, *Heretics and Renegades* (1955); Dutt's review of *1984* was published in the *Daily Worker* (5 January 1955). Both he and Deutscher called *1984* a 'nightmare' and laid the national frenzy about the 'horror plays' of the BBC at the feet of Orwell

[3] George Woodcock endorsed Deutscher's views in Utopias in negative, *Sewanee Review*, 64 (1956) pp 81-97. See also Irving Howe's comparisons among Orwell, Zamyatin and Huxley's *Brave New World* in The fiction of anti-utopia, *New Republic*, Vol. 46 (1962) pp 13-16. Many literary intellectuals – even Orwell's most outspoken admirers such as Woodcock and Howe – were taken in by Deutscher's own 'mystique' of scholarship and erudition, along with his tendency to downplay in his major books – though not in day-to-day journalism – his pro-USSR views and rationalisations of Stalin's crimes. A representative instance of the uncritical, deferential treatment of Deutscher's essay in various collections devoted to Orwell is Irving Howe's *Orwell's Nineteen Eighty-Four: Text, Sources, Criticism* (New York: Harcourt 1982 [1963]), a volume widely adopted in high school and college classrooms of the 1960s through the 1980s. Howe places Deutscher's essay among contributions by the pre-eminent Anglo-American intellectuals and scholars of the day, such as V.S. Pritchett, Lionel Trilling, Woodcock, Bertrand Russell, E.M. Forster, Hannah Arendt and Richard Lowenthal. Introducing Deutscher to the student reader, Howe comments that it 'would seem fair to describe Isaac Deutscher's essay as a serious intellectual attack on *Nineteen Eighty-Four*'. Howe remains studiously impartial and respectful: 'From which point of view does he seem to be writing? Do you accept any of his arguments?'

[4] See Sally Coniam, Orwell and the origins of *Nineteen Eighty-Four*, *Times Literary Supplement*, 31 December 1999

[5] Kathryn Hughes' review of *Wifedom: Mrs Orwell's Invisible Life*, *The Times*, 12 August 2023

[6] *Brisbane Times*, 4 July 2023. It goes unmentioned by the reviewer (and elided in *Wifedom*) that Orwell's 'piss-farting around in the hills of Catalonia' earned him a bullet in the throat. While Eileen certainly exhibited courage and love by following Orwell to Spain, visiting him at the front and managing the office in the Barcelona headquarters of the ILP, it should be mentioned that three Stalinist spies, including Cambridge-educated David Crook, befriended her and managed to photocopy and/or abscond with thousands of valuable documents that placed her husband and other soldiers fighting in the Workers' Party of Marxist Unification (POUM) militia (as well as party members) at considerable risk. She gave Crook free rein of the office, readily accepted his cover story to serve as an office volunteer and regularly left him alone in the office for substantial periods of time at mid-day. Crook took advantage of the trusting nature and Oxbridge nonchalance of Eileen, conducting his espionage with dispatch during her daily lunch hour. Neither *Wifedom* nor the reviews include mention of this lapse at 'the nerve centre'. A touch of Orwell's much-derided 'paranoia' about the machinations of the Stalinists would have served Eileen well here

[7] See Robert McCrum, Genius writer, cruel husband: Why we can never look at George Orwell the same way again, *Independent*, 13 August 2023

[8] Nick Bryant, Playing fast and loose with past, *Sydney Morning Herald*, 29 November 2023. Intended as a critique of Orwell and his seven 'male biographers', the headline is unintentionally ironic. Only uninformed or

ideologically motivated readers would ever regard Eileen as the co-author of *Animal Farm*

⁹ *Wifedom* p. 296

¹⁰ One of them was T.R. Fyvel, who wrote in his *George Orwell: A Personal Memoir* (1982) with admiration for the fable's 'light touch and restraint (almost "unOrwellian")' and notes that 'some of the credit is due to the conversational influence of Eileen and the light touch of her bright humorous intelligence' (p. 138). I agree. Many critics have remarked on Fyvel's astute observation and the wide recognition accorded the comment further testifies to the fact that Eileen has not been ignored nor 'cancelled' by Orwell biographers and scholars. The quotation is also cited in *Wifedom*, but Funder twists it. Eliding Fyvel's explicit reference to Eileen's 'conversational influence', she conjectures that the contribution extended to rewriting the fable (presumably Eileen typed it). She also fails to quote the crucial next sentence: 'All this is just my surmise.' He added that he had no contact with Eileen after the early months of World War II. Instead, Funder suggests that the absence of some recorded statement by Orwell about Eileen's specific contribution exemplifies his 'theft-and-erasure' strategy to cancel her. Moreover, Orwell's humour has generally been overlooked by the critics. Many of his friends from the 1940s had never read *Down and Out in Paris and London*, or many of his book reviews and occasional pieces that repeatedly showed flashes of humour. The idea that Orwell was a gloomy fellow and that *Animal Farm*'s light touch was a departure for him (Funder has called it an 'outlier' for its humour, both in her book and in her book tour stops) is a myth

¹¹ Daniel Siegel (1935-2019) played a little-known and -appreciated role in the history of Orwell's reputation. A prominent book collector of rare books and literary manuscripts from the Romantic era through World War I, he was internationally renowned for his personal library, which contained rare editions of works by Emerson, Whitman and Wilde. The jewel in the collection's crown, however, was Orwell's *Nineteen Eighty-Four*. Siegel was also well-known for his publishing imprint, M. & S. Press, which brought out the edition of the facsimile manuscript of Orwell's novel in the title year, 1984

¹² Such oversights are certainly unfortunate, indeed shoddy, but such slip-ups are in themselves of secondary importance. A few scholarly lapses are well-nigh inevitable when addressing a figure such as Orwell who has attracted such a massive secondary literature. What is deplorable, however, is the vilification of other diligent and responsible scholars on the basis of their allegedly poor scholarship – especially when, ironically, the incendiary allegations ('misogyny', 'sexism') arise from the accusers' own negligent research

¹³ That latter proclivity accounts for the fact that *Wifedom* refers to 'brothels' and 'prostitutes' no less than four dozen times. The 'biography' (conveniently?) omits an index, rendering the tracing of the author's argument more difficult for print readers. Is Funder's *Wifedom* a 'biography'? Not by any standard that most scholars would grant – and revealingly, apparently also not by the author herself. Notably, *Wifedom* is explicitly and aggressively marketed as such by her publisher, treated as such by reviewers and discussed as such by Funder herself on her book tours, though Funder is careful never to use that word in the book to describe what she terms her 'counterfiction'. Her 'counterfiction' advances scenarios that have outraged the surviving family members of the principals involved. For instance, *Wifedom* claims that Celia Kirwan not only had sexual relations with Orwell but also even made the arduous journey to visit him on Jura in the Scottish Hebrides. However, Ariane Bankes, Kirwan's daughter, has stated: 'I know from letters between my mother and her twin sister, Mamaine, who was married to Koestler, that despite Orwell's advances, she never wanted sex with Orwell, and never had any.' Bankes is publishing a memoir of her mother later in 2024 that quotes from this correspondence to rebut *Wifedom*'s contentions. (Viking, the publisher of *Wifedom*, has agreed to print corrections to several errors pointed out by Bankes and others.) Quoted in Richard Brooks,

ARTICLE

Sadistic and misogynistic? Row erupts over sex claims in book about George Orwell's marriage, *Observer*, 11 November 2023

[14] By contrast, regarding Eileen's generous contributions to her brother's scholarship – Eileen not only typed but also heavily edited as well as proof-read Laurence O'Shaughnessy's medical articles and books – I regard it as rather careless or insensitive that he did not publicly acknowledge Eileen's contributions in his acknowledgements. Laurence was an internationally recognised medical researcher and surgeon; Eileen even took dictation from her brother and thereafter wrote it all up in serviceable prose. As Sylvia Topp notes: 'Eileen was on constant call to her brother' before and after her marriage; he never expressed his thanks publicly. Of course, this does not mean that he did not thank her privately, let alone that Eileen was hurt or took offence. She seems to have been proud and gratified to have been so useful to him – and Laurence evidently contributed richly to her life in other concrete ways. By all accounts, their relationship was extremely close throughout their lives. The point is rather a comparative one between Laurence and George Orwell. His critics do him a disservice when they casually equate the two very different categories of writing with two very different sets of literary conventions, namely Orwell's fiction/journalism and Laurence's scholarship (see Topp 2020: 83-84)

[15] Brilliant, but selfish and sexist: A new look at Orwell, *AFR Online*, 22 August 2023 and Jessica Ferri, Was George Orwell's monstrous behavior responsible for his wife's death?, *Los Angeles Times*, 18 August 2023. The headline is unfortunately typical of *Wifedom*'s reception in the mainstream press

[16] Quoted in *AFR Online*. The tribute is by Melbourne novelist Chloe Hooper

[17] Amy Walters, Anna Funder rescues George Orwell's wife Eileen from being 'cancelled by the patriarchy' and reminds us he's a sexual predator, *The Conversation* (Australia), 2 July 2023

[18] *Wifedom* pp 411, 445

[19] One of her Oxford tutors was C.S. Lewis – soon to be a widely selling author of utopias and fantasy fiction – who certainly would also have drawn her attention to Wells if she were not already acquainted with him. For Lewis, as for Orwell, Wells was a hero of his boyhood. Lewis was deeply influenced by Wells, though his Christian convictions clashed with Wells's Darwinian and atheistic outlook and Fabian belief in progress, which Lewis mocked as 'Wellsianity'. (Lewis's *Out of the Silent Planet* is a direct reply to and inversion of Wells's *War of the Worlds*.)

[20] See George Orwell, *Nineteen Eighty-Four: The Facsimile of the Extant Manuscript*; edited by Peter Davison; Preface by Daniel G. Siegel, Weston, MA: M. & S. Press, 1984. I have cited page numbers in the manuscript within the main text. Regrettably, less than half the book survives in Orwell's hand, but this is the only one of Orwell's books for which a manuscript exists. In fact, the manuscript's existence was known years before the publication of the facsimile version. I became aware of it in the early 1980s – before the facsimile version was published – during my research visits to the Orwell Archive; at the request of Sonia Orwell, its owner, Daniel G. Siegel, had deposited a microfilm copy there in 1975. One of the last important acts performed by Ian Angus, in his capacity as the Orwell Archive's first director (1960-1975), was to obtain the manuscript. Siegel had purchased it for $5,000 in June 1969. (Seventeen years earlier, Sonia had donated it to a charity auction, where it fetched the grand sum of £50, equivalent to $140; a few months later, it was sold for $275 to a collector, who owned it until Siegel bought it. Siegel donated it to his alma mater, Brown University, on his death in 2019.)

[21] Consider, for instance, this early version in the facsimile of an important passage in Part Three, section 5, in which Charrington's shop is contrasted with Winston's cubicle in Minitrue and his apartment:

> The weather was baking hot. 1980, if the date was really 1980, was a rainless windless summer of long drought. in the windowless, air-conditioned rooms in the heart of the Ministry [of Truth]. It was terribly cool, but sometimes the hot breath from a memory hole turned one sick and faint, and outside the pavements scorched one's feet and the stench of the tubes at the rush hour was a horror. Winston's flat, immediately under the roof and miserably cold in Winter was like an oven (p. 148).

This passage describing the weather that summer was cut entirely in the published book. Instead, we read: 'The rat had never come back, but the bugs had multiplied hideously in the heat'

[22] Although she also published a pair of poems in the same magazine during high school, that poem is the sole adult publication that bears Eileen's name. Sylvia Topp has speculated that she may have contributed one or more anonymous articles to the London *Evening News*, in November 1926, in December 1928 and in November 1933, respectively. This conjecture lacks, however, any concrete evidence. (The latter article is signed with initials that do not recognisably evoke Eileen's name.) (see Topp 2020: 35-37)

[23] The lone exception is Gordon Bowker's biography (2003: 382). Citing Bowker and Coniam, Angela Smith (*George Orwell Studies*, Vol. 7, No. 1 pp 6-22) writes that 'the poem is now thought to have been influential in Orwell choosing *Nineteen Eighty-Four* as the title to his best-known book'. 'Now thought' by whom? And with what evidence? Those are the compelling questions begged by the passive construction – the use of which, alleges *Wifedom,* is the clever tactic whereby Orwell's biographers have 'canceled' Eileen. Otherwise, Smith's article is a valuable supplement to Topp's biography that enriches our knowledge of Eileen O'Shaughnessy's schooldays and university career

[24] Or an even more worrisome spectre that irresponsible and lavish claims for significance and originality, owing to poor scholarship, predictably set in motion in such cases: namely, an over-reaction. In Eileen's case, such an over-reaction to claims of 'co-authorship' and 'inspiring' *Nineteen Eighty-Four* may both jeopardise the hard-won appreciation of her literary acumen and risk peremptory dismissal of her probable contributions, both editorial and conversational, to Orwell's early ideas for *Nineteen Eighty-Four*

[25] *Wifedom*, p. 28. Despite quoting the poem in its entirety, Funder completely mischaracterises it in order to suggest that the three-stanza poem essentially encapsulates the horrific vision of Orwell's dystopia. Nothing in the poem explicitly deals with grand geopolitical issues such as totalitarianism, dictatorship and global war, though it does have Huxley overtones, as I have suggested. See *Wifedom* pp 422-423

[26] This is a rare instance in which Sylvia Topp may have erred in her judgement about the Eileen-George relationship and mistakenly inflated Eileen's influence on Orwell's work. Unfortunately, no concrete evidence exists that Eileen ever told Orwell about her poem, let alone that he may have remembered it many years later and decided on his novel's title because of it. The idea that the vision in Eileen's poem 'foreshadows Orwell's vision expressed in *1984* of a world where the only accepted thought is prescribed by Big Brother' is misconceived, not least because Eileen's poem ultimately projects an optimistic version of the future. As Topp acknowledges, Eileen seems to have believed in her poem that 'the world would right itself'. Topp also argues that Orwell's first two biographers, Bernard Crick and Michael Shelden, 'weren't aware of the obvious connection between the title of the poem and the title of his great last novel *1984*' because 'Eileen's poem was not discovered until 2001 after many [sic] Orwell biographies had been published'. (Actually, the discovery was made in the late 1990s; it was publicised in British literary circles, including the aforementioned reprint and commentary by Sally Coniam in the *TLS*, in 1999; only two biographies, by Bernard Crick in 1980 and Michael Shelden 1991, had yet been published when the *TLS* article appeared.) Nonetheless, 'with this new knowledge it is hard today

ARTICLE

not to accept that almost final choice of title for his final book was a tacit tribute to Eileen's memory'. That claim goes too far. In point of fact, 'it is hard today not to accept' the likelihood that Orwell probably never remembered the poem on his sickbed in the Scottish Hebrides as he feverishly worked on the novel as the winter of 1948-1949 approached. Certainly Shelden, Meyers, Taylor and even Bowker – not to mention other scholars aware of the poem – never made any such definitive claim, probably because their awareness of the facsimile manuscript of *Nineteen Eighty-Four* sensitised them to Orwell's preoccupation, as his revisions progressed, with choosing dates from the 1980s for his setting. (see Topp 2020 pp 86, 105 and 405)

[27] John Rodden, *The Politics of Literary Reputation: The Making and Claiming of 'St George' Orwell* (New York: Oxford, 1989) pp 225-26

[28] Ibid p. 225

NOTE ON THE CONTRIBUTOR

John Rodden has written widely on George Orwell since the early 1980s. His forthcoming book, *George Orwell: Plagiarist and Predator*, further addresses the now-approaching 'Hundred Years' War' of Orwell vs. the Marxist left.

INTERVIEW

'It's a Completely New Book as Far as I'm Concerned'

George Orwell Studies book reviews' editor Megan Faragher spoke with D.J. Taylor, author of the award-winning *Orwell: The Life* (2003), about his latest book, *Orwell: The New Life*.

MF: If you've read both this book and the original of 2003, you will notice immediately that it's a complete reworking.

DJT: You're right. How I did it was I simply started again from scratch. I went back to my original interview notes from friends of his that I'd interviewed, and I collated the new material. Then I began again, and the only things that survive completely are just one or two of the interleaving essays: 'Orwell and his such-and-such'. But even those have been altered. The obvious one is the essay about Orwell's voice, where some interesting new material has come to light. I can't prove anything, but it does seem as if out there somewhere is a record of Orwell's voice; it's just that it has disappeared again. Other than that, it's a completely new book as far as I'm concerned.

MF: As you approached starting from scratch, what was the principle or philosophy behind re-approaching material that you've worked on before?

DJT: I always give three reasons as to why I decided to do this. One is the volume of new material; certainly, in terms of Orwell's pre-war life, there was enough material to radically redefine and flesh out quite a lot. So, almost certainly in terms of chronology one of the more mundane, bread-and-butter uses of those letters to [his friends] Eleanor [Jaques] and to Brenda [Salkeld] is just showing where he is, what he was doing, how he was spending his time and what he was reading.[1] I think somebody with a more computational approach worked out that there are 85 more pages in the pre-war bit, so there was that aspect.

The second reason is the dwindling band of Orwell survivors. There are only seven people left on the planet now who can actually remember him, and it was important to get hold of them now.

The third reason is – and sorry if this is just an obvious remark – biography never stands still. It's always changing. Your sensibility is changing; the way you regard the person that you're writing the biography about changes. And I found that there were a number of new interpretive techniques that I found very valuable. The one I always instance, obviously, is the Black Lives Matter movement. This was brought home to me in the summer when I was doing a talk in London and a Jamaican came up to me and said: 'You know, that was extremely interesting. My name is Blair.' I looked, and he turned out to be something like the great, great, great grandson of some freed slaves on Orwell's great grandfather's estate in Jamaica, who had taken their former owner's name. Then they were liberated. And there he was. And there Richard Blair [Orwell's son] was as well, and this was absolutely fascinating to have these two people in the same room. So, that's the third reason.

The fourth reason is, of course, my Orwell fixation, which has gone on for nearly half a century and will continue until I die. And so those were the things I sat down thinking: this is why this is being done, this is the *modus operandi*.

'WHAT WAS THE MOST IMPACTFUL NEW MATERIAL?'

MF: As you've mentioned, there are various new tranches of material that you've inserted into the book, including the letters between him and Malcolm Muggeridge and Eleanor Jaques and Brenda Salkeld. As you look back, was there a particular tranche of material that was the most impactful for you as you were putting this together? You talk about the early life being more extended, so what added the most in terms of the new material that you were able to integrate?

DJT: I've never really thought of myself a professional biographer, which may sound odd. I've only ever written about two people, who are Orwell and Thackeray. I do it with a personal enthusiasm, simply because of the love of the person and wanting to write about them. Having said that, I have written group biographies, but that's a rather different thing. There are occasional moments when you suddenly think: 'I am a proper biographer.' And one of them was when the Eleanor [Jaques] letters came to light, because I've been chasing them for years.

I spent ten years on the trail of the Eleanor letters, and then they turned up and led to the discovery of the Brenda letters a little bit later. That was the moment when I suddenly thought: 'You're actually a proper biographer. You're out there looking for stuff; you're finding things; you're doing your work.' And [the letters] do tell us a great deal about Orwell, his specific relationship with

Eleanor, and his approaches to women and his relationships, which were fascinating. But there was a kind of symbolic aspect for me, thinking: 'This is being a biographer, boy! This is kind of getting *on* with it!' So, I think that was probably the moment.

MF: How do you think Orwell's relationship to women informs our understanding of Orwell as a writer?

DJT: It is interesting because the previous absence of material encouraged a male focus. I think that the arrival of women scholars in the field, looking particularly at Orwell's relationships with women, is a good thing, although I must say I have my reservations about the Anna Funder [author of the controversial *Wifedom*] approach. But I think it is valuable.

The discovery, for example, of the letters to Norah Myles; most of our information about Orwell, and *ipso facto* Orwell's dealings with women, came from men. That's just how it was. It's not a conspiracy. It was just how circumstances were, in the literary world, that most of his friends were men. Most of the reminiscences left of him, formal reminiscences, were by men who would simply have seen Eileen in the way that most men did at the time. They would have seen Eileen as an adjunct, and they wouldn't have thought there was anything unusual about Orwell and Eileen's marriage. Obviously, we're applying the standards of the 21st century to a relationship that ended in 1945, but that's inevitable. That's what every generation does. It's like people being horrified about Dickens's marriage, which people at the time weren't horrified with because those were the social mores of the 1840s and 50s. So, I think it's an inevitable thing. And it's a good one, too. On the most basic level, not even going into the gender politics, it gives Orwell's life more of a context than it previously had – just simply seeing the thing in Orwell terms.

And it doesn't apply to Eileen only; it applies to Sonia [Brownell, Orwell's second wife, whom he married just days before he died in January 1950] as well – that endless debate about what were Sonia's motives, what did she think she was doing? In fact, one of the most valuable conversations I think I had about Sonia was with her old friend Janetta Parladé, who died five years ago. I interviewed her a couple of years before she died. This was in connection with my book about the 'lost girls', the literary women of the '40s, and to talk to a woman, albeit one then in her 90s, about Sonia's motivation back in the '40s was fascinating because Janetta was, I think it probably fair to say, her best friend then. And Janetta looked at me and said: 'Oh, it was all about control – with very good motives, you see, of wanting to help.' But again, if you ask women who knew Sonia what her motivation was in wanting to become the second Mrs Orwell, you sometimes get answers which are not satisfactory to 21st century scholars. You get answers like: 'Oh, you know, she wanted to sit at the feet of a great man and help him do his important work.' Now, we may not like that here in 2023, but that does seem to have been a part of her motivation, rightly or wrongly. You get this fascinating interplay of the attitudes of the '40s contrasting with the attitudes of the 2020s and, once the smoke has risen from the battlefield, there sits Sonia and you're trying to work out what it was that made her behave the way that she did.

This is fascinating to me. One of the consequences of that is – and [I think this is so] with Eileen given the interplay of generational forces – ultimately. in some ways, the motivation hangs out of reach. Eileen, for example, is so self-effacing, and those Norah Myles letters are so Delphic, with such thin lines, so witty, so coded, so encrypted because she's writing to a personal friend of longstanding. There are ways in which I hesitate to make a judgement about them. To say that is an abrogation of the biographer's responsibility, but I'm sure you know what I mean by that in terms of not wanting to.

MF: At risk of asking you to pontificate further on Eileen, something that struck me in reading this biography was the treatment of Eileen's work during the war, the frenetic pace of that work, as you described here. This reminded me a lot of Orwell's own treatment of his own work at the expense of his body. I'm curious how you compare their habits in that regard. They seem so similar in a way that struck me anew on reading your book.

'THERE WAS OBVIOUSLY A DEEP AFFINITY BETWEEN ORWELL AND EILEEN'

DJT: They do. There was obviously a deep affinity between them. Eileen was obviously prepared to relegate her own personal importance and her own affairs. There's that terrible story about Eileen running home every day to cook Orwell's lunch, because she thought he was more important than she was. But also realising the situation and being prepared to make jokes about it in a much more circumspect way. There's this sense of selflessness, this sense of attachment, and this sense of being able to see herself in a perspective that most people are unable to do, because they're simply concentrating on themselves. I think all that is admirable on one hand, and it sets you back on the other, because you think: 'How little regard does she have for herself and why couldn't she have fought in her corner?' So, there are all these kinds of conflicting responses. But I agree with you about that. I suppose the fact that they are living their lives in the same way makes me think that the marital bond between them was extremely strong and that both of them knew what they were doing. This is the point I would always make about Eileen: she knew what she was doing. I don't think she was being exploited and I don't think she was being oppressed. I think she had made a decision in the context of the way that married life went on in the 1940s and she stuck by it. We may not find that appropriate by the standards of 2023, but that was her decision and that was how she decided to live her life.

MF: I'd say, as an aside, that is something I think pulls through in *The Lost Girls* for me, in the sense that they were women making decisions about how they wanted to live their lives, which I think was really compelling in both of these books.[2]

DJT: I agree with you, actually. There was a sense in which those girls in the 40s were exploited or allowed themselves to be exploited, or simply the tenor of the times enabled them to be subjugated in ways in which they perhaps weren't aware. But I'm also struck by the fact that to a certain extent, they had agency. I mean, you couldn't read about the life of Barbara Skelton without thinking: 'That woman had agency!' She could make decisions. If she didn't like a man, she'd tell him and throw something at him and storm out of the room. So doormats, they weren't. Janetta, too, was an immensely clever and strong-willed young woman who behaved as she wished to.

MF: I wanted to talk about what you've called the interweaved chapters. I call them the interstitial chapters.

DJT: That's a good description, actually. I call them mini essays, but interstitial chapters is just great...

MF: Yes. Like 'Orwell's face', 'Orwell's voice' and 'Orwellian and rats' in this edition. You maintain those in these books. I'm wondering how those emerged to start with, and what about Orwell makes that particular approach appealing?

DJT: Well, I suppose one reason is simply the search for novelty, in which one wants to do something a bit different, rather than just sticking to the usual chronological progress that biographies habitually consist of. The other reason, though, is I found with Orwell, possibly more so than many another real actual or potential biographical subject, there are aspects of his life and aspects of his psychology that just don't lend themselves to the chronological approach.

So, take Orwell and the working classes, for example. You think: 'This is all fascinating, but how do I get into the chronology? How do I fit it? Do I keep going back to it? Do I give it a couple of pages in the middle of one of the '30s [chapters]?' It seemed to me, twenty years ago, the best way was simply to take a particular subject and write a little essay about it and then fit it in, because it just seemed to me that Orwell was better accommodated by taking that approach than simply slipping in a paragraph here and a paragraph there. It just focuses and concentrates things and it just seemed to be a better way of doing it.

The other thing, too, is that some of those aspects of him, I think, do need extended treatment to make them work. If you're discussing, say, Orwell's attitude to the past, which I got very interested in, it has to have three or four pages. You can't just do it in a couple of paragraphs. It's more complicated than that. It needs a more extensive treatment.

MF: You've added some [more] of those interstitial chapters here, and I'm thinking of the chapters like 'Orwell and his world' and 'Orwell in fiction'. In those, in the ones you've added, I sense this theme of looking at Orwell from the outside – both the outside of readers looking back and thinking about Orwell, but also those around him at the time and how they perceived him. Is that a theme in these new additions?

'THE BOOK IS ABOUT TWO ORWELLIAN MYTHS'

DJT: I would agree with you there. As I say in the book, this is about the two kinds of myth, actually. There are the myths that Orwell propagated about himself, which I think he did almost consciously: the stage management of his life. And then [there are] the myths that are projected around him. I quote, in both books, Malcolm Muggeridge reading the obituaries on the afternoon when he comes back from the funeral and saying that he saw in them how the legend of a man was created.

And as soon as that legend was created, then all Orwell's friends who then made retrospective judgements about him were buying into it, and fashioning what they wrote in terms of the legend that they themselves had had [a part in]. Rayner Heppenstall writes interestingly about this in *Four Absentees* (1960) about an Orwell myth that had been created and he was being asked to contribute to it.[3] Well, why not? Because he'd known him, and his perspective was as valuable as everybody else's. But of course, Heppenstall is contributing to that myth by writing up his account of the occasion when Orwell hit him with the shooting stick. He's writing it up in the context of *Nineteen Eighty-Four* – the sadistic exaltation and so forth. He wouldn't have written like that pre-1949.

So, you've got a kind of parallax view here. You're constantly switching from what people thought about Orwell when they knew him and saw him in the 1930s and 40s, and then what they thought about him afterwards when the legend had time to coalesce and all these other accretions of Orwell's myth and personality had sort of come in. I think I was much more conscious of that this time.

It's like Orwell's reputation, for example. If he had died in the bombing raid in 1941, let us say, we'd have regarded him vastly differently than we do given the fact that he died in 1950. If you're writing about Orwell in the 1930s, you have to remember that he wasn't this celebrated personage. He was actually a very minor literary figure, writing – certainly in his fiction – very old-fashioned books. I like them very much, but they're not on the pace! He's not Hemingway in the 1930s; he's nowhere near! His models are far back in English fictional time at that point.

MF: I wanted to talk about biography, thinking about the stage management, the levels of management of reputation and how the model of biography works in regards to that. You also wrote *On Nineteen Eighty-Four*, which is presented as a biography of a book.[4] I would love to hear you elaborate on that project and how you approached the stakes of doing a biography of a text differently from that of the author or how they're similar.

DJT: Well, it's slightly stagey. It's a very contrived kind of thing. In fact, Abrams [the American publisher] said: 'We're going to do the series, the biographies of books. Would you like to do one?' And I said: 'Well, yes, absolutely!' It was their suggestion. It was their project, which I happily acceded to. I didn't sort of beat myself up theoretically. I didn't think, how do I regard this project on a philosophical basis? I just thought, here's *Nineteen Eighty-Four*. Here's this book. Where can we see the seeds of it in his life? Where did it come from? Then, when he was writing it, how did he write it? And then, thirdly, what happened afterwards? So, there was no great theoretical debate going on. I tend to approach all these things in a rather sort of pragmatic way.

MF: You've also been doing the annotations for Orwell's six novels for the Constable editions. Did doing any of that work impact the *New Life* in any way that was unexpected?

DJT: Absolutely. Doing the annotations was my first lockdown project in the spring of 2020. Here in England – or the remote eastern part of England in which I live – there was nothing for my wife and I to do, except we went around distributing food parcels two afternoons a week. Apart from that, there was nothing to do, nobody to see. So I sat down, I went through, and I did all six books in two or three months. I used localised research that I've been doing. For example, with *A Clergyman's Daughter* I've done a lot of work in Southwold, trying to identify people and places in the book and make connections between fictional portraits and possible models and all that was very fruitful. By the time I'd done all of those, which was then the autumn of 2020, I was beginning to think about the writing of the book itself. I began writing the actual book in April of 2021. So, all of that was an invaluable kind of rehearsal for the writing of the biography.

ORWELL'S LOVE OF THE NATURAL WORLD

MF: I want to go back to the interstitial chapters and, I guess, also things that you do in remote areas. I was thinking of the 'Orwell among the toads' chapter: it strikes me as kind of sharing some similarities with something like Rebecca Solnit's *Orwell's Roses*, and this increased focus on Orwell as this lover of the natural world, which seems relatively renewed as of late. I wonder what you think of that focus on those more agrarian senses of Orwell adds to our understanding of him.

DJT: Well, it's interesting because this rural side is evident in everything that he wrote, and I'm especially interested in the conflation of his feelings for nature and his feelings for women. The obvious thing is the *al fresco* scenes in *Nineteen Eighty-Four*. But you see this in *Burmese Days*. You see it in *Keep the Aspidistra Flying*. If there's a woman involved in something that's going on in the country, then the pace of the writing quickens up. It has a galvanic effect on him. So, I was interested in this – as to where that came from. This is very interesting in the context that you were just asking about, working on the six novels and the path up to *Nineteen Eighty-Four*.

There's always, as you know, been this great debate as to who is Julia [Winston Smith's secret lover]. Is she Sonia? It seems to me that the natural world – stroke – romantic interest conflation goes all the way back to Jacintha Buddicom. It was Jacintha who thought she was traduced by the Julia scenes in *Nineteen Eighty-Four*. But I was struck by the similarities of some of the language used in the Julia scenes; I found what I thought were traces in some of the early letters to Eleanor [Jaques] from 1932. So, it does seem to me to be a constant motif with Orwell. My belief about Julia, as I say in the book, is that she's a composite figure. She's not based on any particular person. She's bringing together all kinds of different sort of stimuli from Orwell's past lives.

MF: Thanks. I want you to also talk a little bit about Orwell's working life. He's the writer. He's the reviewer. It always struck me that it seems the time he was the most flush was in Burma and the BBC. Arguably both were very bad for his health, but they seemed to provide him some money. What strikes you when you think about the writer as worker or as employee, just kind of making ends meet?

DJT: This is the side of Orwell that I've always responded to and been very sympathetic to because he was the consummate freelance. Obviously, I know he was employed at the BBC for two and a half years, but he's one of those people who, you know, writes to live and he lives to write. I've always had an affinity with writers who do that, from Thackeray to Evelyn Waugh to whoever, because, by upbringing or inclination, I'm what they call the lower middle-class Puritan here in the UK. It's the idea that you've got to keep going and work is a virtuous thing. You don't sit around. You're not constantly thinking: 'Oh, when can I stop work and do something for pleasure?' [Work's] a compulsion. And I've always had a compulsion to write. The volume of Orwell's journalism in the Peter Davison [20-volume *Complete Works*] edition that I feel the most affinity for is the one that's called *Smothered Under Journalism*. There he is. He's written *Animal Farm*. He's become a big success. He's actually made some money. He's got *Nineteen Eighty-Four* incubating. His health is declining, but he comes back to London for the winter of 1946-1947, freezing cold, terrible – and he writes three pieces of journalism a week! He doesn't have to do it, but he does because he's driven to do it. And, rightly or wrongly, I always feel very sympathetic towards that. There have been possibly too many writers for me in recent times who've been provided with the means of writing – not very much and not very often – but sitting there, not exactly in ivory towers, but living the leisurely writerly life. You write one novel every two or three years or something. That's not being a writer to me.

Orwell's always down at the coalface. As a habitual freelance myself, one of the essays that I love the most is 'Confessions of a book reviewer'. It's not Orwell; it's not a faithful portrait of him, but it's near enough. It projects certain aspects of his own 30s life seriously enough to make you really think about the connections between the two. I love that essay. It doesn't correspond to my own experience of 50-60 years later, but close enough. You remember: the starving hack unwrapping a parcel of five completely unrelated and unsuitable books, which he despairs over. I remember when I was in my 20s, reviewing novels for the London *Evening Standard*. And again, you would have 500 words, you'd be sent four novels, all completely different from each other, of varying degrees of quality. And you had to write a paragraph that connected them to each other. So, you had to find connections with them that weren't there. It was just desperate, desperate work and there no subediting went into it! If a paragraph needed to go, the editor would just cut off the last paragraph of the review. So, I have great empathy and affinity for that sort of thing and the struggles of the early part of his career. It makes me like him more as a person, the fact that he went through that, that he had to struggle. Even towards the end of his life there's a letter to David Astor [his friend, editor of *The Observer*], I think from the very end of 1948 or beginning of 1949, where he's just literally collapsed, having finished *Nineteen Eighty-Four*, and he's agreed to review some books for *The Observer*. He's fiercely saying: 'I'm really sorry. I've got one of the books, but I just can't do the other one.' And he's obviously really worrying about it. It's traumatising him as much as his illness. And you think to yourself, he didn't really have to bother. He was George Orwell! He had just written *Nineteen Eighty-Four*! Who cares about this piece for *The Observer*? But he worried about it because he'd spent 16 or 17 years doing that sort of journalism, and he didn't want to disappoint his commissioning editor.

HOW ORWELL'S BOOK REVIEWING INFLUENCED *NINETEEN EIGHTY-FOUR*

MF: I want to follow up by talking about the reviews a little more. I was watching an interview that you did with The Orwell Society and you mentioned about the incubatory period for *Nineteen Eighty-Four* and the extension of it. I think of the Tehran conference as being one impact, but also these reviews – I think of James Burnham's review. And I wonder if you could talk a little bit on the extended production of *Nineteen Eighty-Four* in relationship to his reviewing and this other work he's doing.

DJT: I find that is one of the reasons, obviously, that it took so long to write was waning powers. His health was declining. He found it more difficult to write at the pace that he'd usually written at. The other thing was that he hadn't worked out the precise details of *Nineteen Eighty-Four* and its intellectual background. So it is remarkable the run of essays and reviews that he wrote between 1945 and 1947, all of which turn out to have some bearing on the book. There's the James Burnham essay, to which you refer. There's his first reading of Zamyatin's *We*, which produces this extraordinary review in 1946. And very significant, to me, is 'You and the atom bomb' from the autumn of 1945, which is written only a few weeks after the descent of the bombs on Hiroshima and Nagasaki and develops the zones of influence idea, which he got from the Tehran conference. This is developed by 'You and the atom bomb'. Then, of course, there's 'Politics and the English language', another hugely significant influence.

In some ways, as I think I've said before, the trail goes back further than that. And some of the roots of *Nineteen Eighty-Four* lie in that round-up review of dystopian fiction that he does in 1940, where he writes about [Aldous] Huxley and Ernest Bramah and [H.G] Wells, and makes what I think is a fantastically interesting point that connects him up to [George] Gissing, whose truth trail runs through the biography: if there's going to be fascism, then you have to look at the lower-middle classes, because they've got more to lose from a socialist revolution than anybody else, and they're more likely to be in favour of authoritarianism.

MF: I want to return to something we started talking about at the beginning, which is the resurgence in Orwell and the interest in Orwell. Obviously, there's twenty years between *The Life* and *The New Life*, which is a convenient marker of time more than anything. I wonder what you've noticed about the transformation in interest in Orwell or criticism of Orwell in that time period? What has changed?

DJT: It's very opportune that you should ask that because I've just written a supplementary chapter – an afterword – for the paperback, which is coming out in the U.K. in the spring ... and one of the points I make is that when I started working on Orwell back in the 1990s, there was such a thing as Orwell Studies. Now there's an Orwell industry, and the Orwell industry, in some ways, is bad news for a ... generalist like myself, because it means that every area of Orwell's work has got some specialist involved in it who probably knows more about it than you do. So, this could be slightly worrying, but there is this vast increase in interest.

I've done a lot of blogger interviews and Zoom talks with American interviewers in the last six months. I've been to America twice to promote the book at literary festivals and things like that. I've noticed that in the places I've been to in America, I am confronted with what I would call exemplary liberal audiences – this is places like Boston and Rhode Island, upstate New York. But one would get these interview requests and – not knowing huge amounts about the milieu – I would say to my American publicist: 'Oh, so-and-so have just asked me to do an interview.' And they'd say: 'But you need to be careful because they're associated with the *National Review*.' So there's an awful lot of what we'll call the neo-con right very interested in Orwell at the moment, and they're using him in just the same way that the right used *Nineteen Eighty-Four* in the 1950s ... and which Orwell himself predicted before he died. They're using him as a stick to beat the left. In the autumn, every few days I'd be Googling away, as writers do. And I'd find some long, incredibly enthusiastic review in some American publications that I wasn't really aware of. And I'd think: 'Oh yes, you're one of *those* publications.' You would find the book reviewed in a right-wing religious publication where the reviewer would say: 'The only thing that is missing from Mr Orwell's view of the world is belief in God.' I make the point that Orwell's ideal would have been a secularism that embodied the moral precepts of Christianity. In other words, Christianity without the afterlife was what he was looking towards.

Of course, no English reviewer would ever write anything like that. We just don't have the same kinds of media over here. Of course, I'm absolutely just delighted that people like the book and respond to it. But there were occasions reading these reviews when I thought I was collateral in a war that I didn't realise was being fought, if you know what I mean. Not so much over here. There are one or two publications like that in the UK, but not many of them where Orwell is being used as a broom to dust away various bits of left-wing debris that annoyed the reviewer. In fact, do you know Sandra Newman, who wrote what I thought was a very good novel, *Julia*?[5]

MF: Yes.

DJT: I understand she's written a piece in *The Washington Post* recently wondering whether Orwell is going to get cancelled for objectionable views about this, that or the other.[6] Now, my own view is that Orwell, hopefully, is too big for that kind of sniping. Whatever mud you throw at him, not very much of it sticks. I don't think Orwell will be cancelled. But I think that people are going to say foolish things about him. Are going to see him in absurd contexts or criticise him for failings that he couldn't possibly have been aware of.

You will have noticed there is an essay [in the book] – in fact, an expanded version of one of the original essays – 'Orwell and the Jews'. Obviously, there are some indefensible things said about Jewish people in the 1930s novels but, however offensive, they are no different than the offensive things that were written down by virtually every English novelist writing in the 1930s. And, however much we may deplore them, you have to see them in the context of their time. This gets personal for me. My father, for example, who was born in 1921, used to make what would now be called Jewish jokes. And my father spent five years fighting against fascism. So, you have to see these things contextually, I think.

Eliot, Priestley, Waugh, Greene, everybody – the novels of the 1930s are full of what would now be called antisemitism. In the 1930s, they called it Jew-baiting, and they maintained that there was a difference between the two. Whether there was or not before the Holocaust, I don't know. I'm a great fan of those great sprawling American naturalist novels of the 1920s and 1930s, and they are full of [such] remarks. So, to sit there, censoriously, 100 years later, and say: 'Orwell was so dreadful! We can never forgive what Orwell wrote about....' I can see the concern of a modern sensibility coming across some of the stuff, say, in *Down and Out in Paris and London*. But I think, ultimately you can defend Orwell convincingly from that, simply because of his attempts later on in his career to make reparations. I'm conscious, in the last five years [of his life], of him deliberately trying to make amends for previous failings once his Jewish friend Tosco Fyvel pointed them out to him in 1945. It's a very difficult and contested area, in which one fears to tread ... but it's another aspect of Orwell that has to be addressed by the modern critic, like Orwell's attitude to homosexuals, which I also devote a chapter to.

ORWELL AS A 'FLOATING SIGNIFIER'

MF: As you point out very usefully in the Introduction, one of the reasons for Orwell's semi-permanence is this aspect of him as a 'floating signifier'. But then he's misused in various contexts in the 1950s and now we see the same resurgence of this false appropriation.

DJT: It's a consequence of attaining a kind of ubiquity that so few writers managed to do. I first started thinking about this, not in the context of Orwell, but in the context of Conan Doyle and Sherlock Holmes ten years ago. Somebody then had written another Sherlock Holmes book: it may have been Anthony Horowitz. A friend of mine at *The Wall Street Journal* said: 'We'd like to write a bit not just about this book but about the whole context and the Holmes industry and this kind of thing.' And some intern at *The Wall Street Journal* sent me every book that they could find on the Amazon catalogue that had something to do with Conan Doyle and Holmes. It was utterly bizarre, because there were not only all these new adventures that he'd taken part in, but there were other writers whose world he was prying into. So, people had written Sherlock Holmes meets H.P. Lovecraft. It was virtually Holmes in *Star Trek*, that kind of thing. When I'd read them, I thought – actually, Sherlock Holmes has no reality anymore. He's just so big that he's gone out there and he's doing things that would be completely alien to his creator and, in fact, have nothing to do with the things that he did in his fictional life. It strikes me that Orwell has reached that level of magnificence. In the U.K., with the copyright restrictions having gone, the Orwell spin-off novels have now started. Paul Theroux's got one out in the spring about Orwell in Burma.[7] There was the *Julia* novel. I thought *Julia* was very good, actually. But you can see that the more and more this happens, the less and less those books all have to do with Orwell.

I've just read a novel by a man called Peter Hodgkinson, published here, which is about Orwell's time at the BBC.[8] It's *Orwell Calling*. And it turns into a kind of murder mystery. And you think: 'What's that got to do with Orwell?' And the answer is nothing. But Orwell has become so big that he's going to attract this kind of treatment now and go on being extrapolated and reinvented. The man himself, and the books, are beginning to be rather a rather long way behind all this.

So – and I think this is more connected with what we were talking about just now about Orwell Studies mutating into the Orwell industry – since I first started working, what I call the microbiographers have set to work. There are people writing whole books about, say, Orwell in Burma. Now, as you know, we know virtually nothing about Orwell in Burma. ... But there are people going to be writing whole books about this. And you have to ask yourself: what are they going to be writing about? With what information? What data are they going to be basing this stuff [on]? I'm not disparaging the work of anybody who sets out to write about Orwell. But, as is always the case with these things, you just wonder where it's going to end. If you want to make a comparison with pop music, let's take *The Beatles*. Somebody just published a biography of one of the Beatles' personal assistants. Where will it end? Will there be biographies of all Paul McCartney's family? I contemplate the phenomenon with interest.

- D.J. Taylor's next book, *Who is Big Brother?: A Reader's Guide to George Orwell*, is being published by Yale University Press this spring.

NOTES

[1] https://blogs.ucl.ac.uk/special-collections/2023/06/28/brenda-salkeld-and-eleanor-jacques-the-lost-letters-of-george-orwell/

[2] D.J. Taylor, *The Lost Girls*, London: Constable, 2019

[3] Rayner Heppenstall, *Four Absentees*, London: Barrie & Rockliff, 1960

[4] D.J. Taylor, *On Nineteen Eighty-Four*, New York: Abrams, 2019

[5] Sandra Newman, *Julia*, New York: Mariner, 2023

[6] Sandra Newman, Now right-wing, anti-'woke' doublethink has come for George Orwell, *Washington Post*, 12 December 2023. https://www.washingtonpost.com/opinions/2023/12/12/orwellian-criticism-right-wing/

[7] Paul Theroux, *Burma Sahib*, London: Penguin, 2024. https://www.penguin.co.uk/books/455643/burma-sahib-by-theroux-paul/9780241633342

[8] Peter Hodgkinson, *Orwell Calling*, Peancobooks, 2022

BOOK REVIEWS

Beasts of England

Adam Biles

Norwich, Galley Beggar Press, 2023 pp 272

ISBN: 9781913111458 (pbk)

'The creatures outside looked from pig to man, and from man to pig, and from pig to man again: but already it was impossible to say which was which' (*CWGO* VIII: 95). *Animal Farm* is the only one of Orwell's fictions that is perfectly crafted. Its concision and precision pack a real punch, and its memorable ending locks in the tale in the most dramatic – and watertight – way. You can only imagine the words THE END following in large type. It is the end of the story, of the revolution and of the argument. What more could there possibly be to say?

Adam Biles has an answer. His new novel *Beasts of England* imagines a future for Animal Farm, which has reverted to its pre-revolutionary name, Manor Farm. All but one of the animals we met in *Animal Farm* have passed on, and their descendants have been joined by a wider cast of characters, the pigs and cows and sheep of the traditional English farmyard that Orwell imagined (and remembered) now supplemented by more exotic company, including alpacas, geckos and pelicans. Devious and cruel humans prowl around the farm's borders as before. Most of Biles's beasts exhibit a sweet but dangerous gullibility and a fatally short memory, like Orwell's animals. The dangers that beset them in the twenty-first century are different, but seem to be herding them – though the ending of Biles's fable has a measure of ambiguity – towards a similar political catastrophe.

What has happened? The segue between *Animal Farm* and *Beasts of England* is accomplished as the book opens with the reproduction of a story in the local newspaper, the *Willingdon Courier*, reporting the re-election of the pig Buttercup as First Beast, and including a brief recapitulation of the farm's recent past. The historical exposition is a bit shifty:

> After Napoleon [the 'despotic porker' of Orwell's tale] was shipped off to the great knacker in the sky, Manor Farm lived through many shaky years before a 'Council of Animals' was established and the first 'Choozin' held. It then took almost

another decade for Manor Farm's proud and suspicious beasts to take their rightful place at the heart of the Wealden Union of Farmers (WUF).... (p. 7).

It's not very clear how the farm escaped from the stranglehold of Napoleon's porcine tyranny to become a democratic two-party state. And no wonder. The model for the story of *Animal Farm* is, as everyone knows, the history of the Soviet Union, and it's doubtful if Orwell could imagine, in 1944, how Stalin's regime could ever evolve or be overthrown. More seriously still, Biles shifts the allegorical base of the tale from Stalinist Russia to contemporary Britain, a country that by no means shares the past envisaged in *Animal Farm* or, most likely, the future. So the first move of *Beasts of England* is to wrench Orwell's fable out of the history that gave it meaning, into a modernity of a kind that it never envisaged. This creates problems that will come back to haunt Biles's allegory, for all its ingenuity.

Ingenious it certainly is. Bipedal pigs still make up the governing class on the farm and compete in elections to form a majority in the somewhat shaky democratic Council of Animals. There are two political parties. Buttercup is the leader of the progressive Animalists and is sitting on a handsome majority when the action begins. The opposition Jonesist party – traditionalist, deferential to humans, fiscally conservative, suspicious of foreigners – is led by Ribbons, a handsome and complacent young boar. The Jonesists look back with nostalgia to the time of their great leader Traviata, a sow whose policies had allowed the pigs and dogs to enrich themselves while the rest of the farm went into decline. Biles doesn't need to depict Traviata with a handbag to help us get our bearings on all this.

A nice touch is the conversion of the farm into the South of England's Premium Petting Zoo. The famous windmill is still working, just, but the productive economy of Animal Farm has otherwise become entirely service-based, relying on the provision of tourist entertainment ('Ride the mule cart! Meet the llamas! Gaze at the gravity-defying geckos!' (p. 7)) and the proceeds of the gift shop. With this has come a steady debasement of the culture of the farm, and the beginnings of a serious corruption of its politics and spoliation of its natural environment. These worrying developments have made Manor Farm vulnerable to a series of ailments that we will find familiar: tribal divisions, populist demagoguery and xenophobia, the latter expressed in a campaign to leave the WUF.

The first sign of trouble to come is the inexplicable arrival of flocks of starlings. Innocuous at first, these birds proliferate at alarming speed and intrude into every level of animal life. They gossip, squabble, make a lot of noise and soon are to be seen alighting on the shoulders of the resident animals to impart to them a version of the news. Before long, nobody is paying much attention to the magpies, the traditional media of information on the farm. With their murmurations in the sky, the starlings seem even to be able to form moving pictures conveying rumour or propaganda. Later it emerges that somebody is introducing mechanical starlings into the flock, with the purpose of deliberately propagating false news. Before long the poor animals, most of them not intellectually gifted in the first place, are hopelessly confused as to what is real and what isn't. The confusion is exemplified when, at harvest time, the mischievous starlings ensure that apples and pears get mixed up in their barrels and nobody can tell which is which.

> As the apple-picking (that's to say pear-picking) season concluded several weeks before the pear-picking (that's to say apple-picking) season, a van arrived to collect the apples (that's to say pears) and take them off to market before they rotted (p. 34).

'Apples? Pears? Who cares?', says Martha the goose (p. 38). But while the animals are settling into their bamboozlement, they are puzzled to learn that their wages have been delayed.

Orwell would have admired the allegorical trope of the starlings. It is at least arguable that the twittering proliferation of social media is a major factor in the debasement of political life in our century, and the weakening of a shared trust in what we are told by sources that used to be thought authoritative. If information is like a supermarket of competing products where we can pick and choose to believe the items that suit or excite us, or confirm our existing prejudices, we are all left open to the most blatant manipulation of opinion. Returning from the Spanish Civil War, Orwell was especially alert to the way lies were being shamelessly peddled, by propagandists on both sides. 'I am willing to believe that history is for the most part inaccurate and biased,' he wrote in 'Looking Back on the Spanish War', 'but what is peculiar to our own age is the abandonment of the idea that history *could* be truthfully written' (*CWGO* XIII: 504).

Orwell worried that the very concept of objective truth might be fading out of the world. This perception plays out in *Nineteen Eighty-Four*, where people rely on the government to remind them if they are at war with Eastasia or Eurasia, and hardly notice when the answer changes. But back in *Keep the Aspidistra Flying* (1936), Orwell was already concerned with the mendacity and cynicism by which the public was duped by retail corporations and the advertising industry: capitalism itself was just as capable of telling lies as the political ideologies of left and right. In this sense, the New

Albion Advertising Agency – a name as utopian as *Animal Farm!* – is the intertextual ancestor of Biles's murmurations of starlings. Truth is hard enough to discern, but harder when irresponsible agents muddy the waters.

Allegory, however, is not infinitely elastic. At a later 'Choozin', the new Animalist leader, Jumbo (a 'dangerous liar'), is pitted against the new Jonesist leader, Pearl (a 'deranged fantasist') (p. 174). Most of us could probably identify these party leaders, put a date on this election and predict the winner. Jumbo is a cynical shock-headed crowd-pleaser; the voters love him. Pearl is an earnest ideologue, politically naïve. He believes irrationally in a non-existent Sugarcandy Mountain. Hopeless at campaigning in the Choozin, instead he persuades his followers to try to excavate this mountain from where he believes it to be buried, under a spinney, with catastrophic consequences for the dormice who live there. In other words, the Animalists dig a hole for themselves. I think I can decode the allegory of the dormice (it seems to have to do with the alleged antisemitism that alienated many British Jews and discredited the Labour Party), but it's far too complex to work as an allegory, and if non-allegorical, it's simply bizarre. Meanwhile, with his divisive populist policies and a whole raft of empty promises, Jumbo wins the election trotters-down.

In this confusion, what could save the animals of Manor Farm? One answer might be a brave cohort of dissidents, determined to seek out the truth and resist the rising and sinister power of Jumbo and his pigs (and men). This cohort exists, in the shape of individual heroes: Martha and Duke the geese, Cassie the mule – her name is short for Cassandra, which is ominous, but she has heroic pedigree, being the daughter of the donkey Benjamin from *Animal Farm* – and later Cosmo the tawny owl. But they are hardly a match for the forces ranged against them.

The other bulwark against injustice and tyranny is the law. In Orwell's novel, we watched the laws of Animalism being gradually altered and perverted, 'All animals are equal' acquiring the brilliant qualification 'but some animals are more equal than others' (*CWGO* VIII: 90). In Manor Farm, the rot has already set in in the first chapter, where the original axiom has now become 'All animals are more equal than others' (p. 16). This may indicate that the residents of the farm will swallow any nonsense, but it lacks the deep wit of Orwell's traduced motto. Meanwhile 'Beasts of England', the revolutionary anthem taught by old Major to his neighbours in *Animal Farm*, is also perverted, so that each time it is sung the singers notice (or don't notice) that the words have been altered to fit the evolving political situation.

As the story proceeds, and becomes more complex, the allegory becomes harder and harder to manage. There are more characters, indeed more species, in *Beasts of England* than in its Orwellian model. What Orwell had learned from Jonathan Swift was that satirical allegory has to maintain a simplicity in order to pack a punch. In this interest, he had worked hard to keep the psychology of his animals both elementary and external. They have acute senses, and some capacity for memory, but he almost never shows them thinking about things. Unlike Orwell, it is tempting to say, Biles is too much of a novelist to maintain this distance. His animals and birds have a private and even intellectual life. They have interiority.

Martha the goose, in particular – though in most respects she is a sort of Everybird – struggles to understand her world in the hope of being able to change it. For this she needs powers that Orwell denied his beasts. At one stage we see her reading an old newspaper, excavated from the rubbish heap, to learn about the past of Manor Farm. The cantankerous Duke, a sort of investigative journalist among geese, takes to drawing increasingly complicated squiggles in the mud by the pond: the squiggles are a code for his discoveries about the toxicity of the pond water which is poisoning the animals, but it is beyond the wit of Cassie to understand this. His last words to Cassie, before he suffers the familiar fate of investigative journalists in a repressive regime, are 'Pry on!' (p. 160). She takes this as encouragement to continue her own investigations, but it later emerges he was actually warning her of the prions, the pathogenic agents in the water. This is desperately clumsy and over-elaborate.

As you can see from *Feeding Time* (Galley Beggar Press, 2016), Biles is a gifted, witty and innovative novelist. This means he always wants to know more about his characters: he can't leave them alone. As the story proceeds, it starts to sound less like an animal allegory (still less a fairy story, as Orwell described *Animal Farm*) and more like a novel about characters who happen not to be humans. Cassie's terrible discoveries late in the tale could almost be out of a science-fiction thriller. It is the helplessness of Orwell's animals that makes their lives moving. In *Beasts of England*, there is a developing awareness of what's being done to them, and with it the stirrings of revolt.

At the end, when a character from *Animal Farm* surprisingly appears (no spoilers here), he seems to become the focus for a possible resistance. It is a resistance lodged in historical memory, loyalty to loved ones and the old ways. For a moment I was reminded of the last act of Jez Butterworth's extraordinary play *Jerusalem* (2009), another drama where revolt arises from a kind of English pastoral and the common experience. It is very moving. Is something changing at last? 'No, it wasn't all of the starlings, and it wasn't all of the animals. But it was some. And some, at least, was a start' (p. 272). It's a start which Orwell did not feel able to allow his beasts at the end of *Animal Farm*.

Three cheers for the independent publisher, Galley Beggar Press, who can be found at www.galleybeggar.co.uk.

Douglas Kerr,
Birkbeck College, University of London

The Socialist Patriot: George Orwell and War

Peter Stansky

Stanford University Press, Stanford, 2023 pp 130

ISBN: 9781503635494 (pbk)

At a time when anarcho-capitalists casually use the word 'Orwellian' to attack market regulations and social programmes as authoritarian, it is crucial to emphasise that Orwell, when it came to economic policies, was unequivocally a socialist. In an era when right-wing activists fuel nationalist sentiments by constructing a caricature of 'socialism' as fundamentally antithetical to the nation state, it is timely to highlight the tradition of socialist patriotism to which Orwell belonged. Peter Stansky's *The Socialist Patriot*, besides sporadic references to how the rise of right-wing populism and the surveillance state spiked the sales of Orwell's later fiction, does not delve into the contemporary uses and abuses of Orwell or the political relevance of his work. As the title suggests, however, the book makes a case for the potential virtues of Orwell's socialist patriotism for the present – how marketable would it have been, among the book's intended audience, to label the blend of Orwell's temperament and politics as, for instance, 'Tory Socialism'?

As much as it is important to reclaim Orwell as part of the left, it is unlikely whether nostalgia for Orwell's socialist patriotism can help revitalise the socialist tradition or save us from the political crises of the present. For Orwell, as Stansky eloquently reconstructs, socialist patriotism was, far from being paradoxical, a necessity. For a period, Orwell believed that England could only emerge victorious in the war if it underwent a socialist revolution. After the war, he naturally reconsidered this stance but persisted in the belief that some form of socialist transformation was needed to prevent his country, and the entire West, from succumbing to totalitarianism. Thus, he believed that for England to remain England, paradoxically it should be radically transformed. Orwell, however, was concerned far less with what this transformation entailed than with how the dominant attitude among left-wing intellectuals alienated the masses and thereby hindered a socialist transformation.

As Stansky correctly observes, Orwell's attempt to blend socialism and patriotism reflected 'his intense love of his country' – a commitment to keep England essentially the same by radically transforming it (p. 54). Besides this commitment, however, Orwell's socialist patriotism was a response to what he perceived as the left wing intellectuals' disregard for an innate sense of belonging in human nature. As Stansky remarks, Orwell romanticised 'the English empirical tradition' over more theoretical ways of thinking, which he associated with the middle class intelligentsia and which he thought could lead to totalitarianism (p. 67). But there is often too much emphasis laid on Orwell's aversion to philosophy. Much like many other anti-Stalinist intellectuals in the Anglophone world, Orwell obsessed over what he understood to be a philosophical naivety among more progressive liberals, whom he labelled as 'dreary tribe of high-minded women and sandal-wearers and bearded fruit-juice drinkers who come flocking towards the smell of "progress" like bluebottles to a dead cat' (Orwell 2021 [1937]: 125). These were, in Orwell's view, outcasts who alienated the more 'normal' masses of people from socialist ideas.

Of course, much could be speculated about the failure of socialist movements in the West, and perhaps a cultural divide was, as Orwell thought, a key part of this failure. It remains unclear, though, how Orwell's obsession with the attitudes of the intelligentsia and other marginalised groups would contribute to forming a robust socialist movement. Instead, it seems that this obsession with cultural and philosophical matters provided ammunition to those in his opposite political camp, diverting attention from economic and political issues. Many conservative socialists did, in fact, slowly migrate to the opposite political camp. We can only speculate what Orwell would have done, had he lived fifteen or twenty years longer, witnessing the emergence of an even more culturally rebellious left.

While *The Socialist Patriot* does not include a critical evaluation of Orwell's socialist patriotism, it does offer an engaging account of its biographical roots. The book's subtitle, *George Orwell and War*, could be a bit misleading, as it creates an expectation for a strong theoretical thesis about the role of war in Orwell's work. Fortunately, the book does not propose 'war' as a key concept that can resolve Orwell's complexities. Rather, Stansky uses the four wars which impacted Orwell's life – the First World War, the Spanish

BOOK REVIEW

Civil War, the Second World War and the Cold War – as a means of structuring his narrative and contextualising Orwell within specific historical contexts in which he grew up and lived. Of these, perhaps the most original are Stansky's second and first chapters, on the First World War and the period before it – because much more has been said, including by Orwell himself, about the Spanish Civil War and the Second World War, as well as the post-war landscape in which *Nineteen Eighty-Four* (1949) appeared.

This short book captures Stansky's decades-long scholarship on Orwell, but it is written in an accessible and engaging way, free from academic jargon and scholarly pretensions. Particularly enjoyable is Stansky's Preface, where he candidly recounts the origins of his own fascination with Orwell and its evolution into an academic career. Stansky became an Orwell scholar at a time when researching Orwell still involved extensive archival research and exciting interviews with individuals who knew him firsthand. The accumulated volume of secondary literature on Orwell since then is colossal, and yet it remains enjoyable to write about the English author – as Stansky himself continues to do.

Orwell famously did not want any biographies of him to be published – a wish that was somewhat honoured until, incidentally, *The Unknown Orwell* by Stansky and William Abrahams appeared in 1972. Maybe Orwell's wish was more of a performative gesture. He could probably foresee that biographies of him would be published, whether he liked it or not. Besides, Orwell himself wrote many biographically informed accounts of other authors. In any case, should Orwell have come across *The Socialist Patriot*, he would at least appreciate that Stansky has adhered to his rules of composition, producing an approachable and entertaining text, free from unnecessary abstractions.

REFERENCE

Orwell, George (2021 [1937]) *The Road to Wigan Pier*, Oxford: Oxford University Press

Mir Ali Hosseini,
University of Regensburg

The Never End: The Other Orwell, the Cold War, the CIA, MI6 and the Origin of *Animal Farm*

John Reed

Palgrave Macmillan, Basingstoke, 2023 pp 199

ISBN: 9789819907640 (hbk); 9789819907656 (e-book)

BOOK REVIEW

This volume is a collection of some of the writings and interviews that John Reed has devoted to the attempted demolition of George Orwell's reputation over the last twenty years. He acknowledges that, looking back, some of the early pieces strike him as 'screechy, high-pitched in their rage', but in his defence he was trying to establish that Orwell 'wasn't the benevolent white savior that we'd made him out to be' (p. 2). After all, Reed had *Animal Farm*'s message that 'all revolutions are destined to fail' relentlessly drummed into him at school without being told that the book's author had 'been complicit with the CIA' (p. 2). To show any revolutionary impulse at school had inevitably been met with 'brays of "Four legs good, two legs bad"' (p. 108).

His experience of the book's use at school seems to have had a profound impact on him; then there was his encounter with Christopher Hitchens. In the immediate aftermath of the 9/11 terrorist attack, Reed wrote a sequel to *Animal Farm* chronicling Snowball's return after Napoleon's death. In his *Snowball's Chance*, Reed has Snowball effecting the restoration of capitalism and setting Manor Farm down a road that leads to, indeed provokes, its own 9/11 attack. This book led to difficulties with the Orwell Estate and to clashes with Christopher Hitchens who was, at the time, posing as Orwell's great champion, if not his successor. Reed describes Hitchens as 'the grand Poohbah of the cult of Orwell' (p. 109).

Now as someone who has himself clashed with Hitchens, in my case with regard to the poet Philip Larkin, my own view of the man is that he was a posh charlatan who relentlessly plagiarised other people's work but got away with it because of his way with words and his ability to turn on the charm (Newsinger 1993a and 1993b; Hitchens 1993). Reed makes the mistake in his diatribes of even blaming Orwell for Hitchens, which is surely a step too far.

Reed pulls together a familiar catalogue of Orwell's faults and crimes: his 'abuse of Socialists … was as vicious as any Tory' (p. 9), and his journalism and personal writing was in the main 'whining and stinking of body odor. He was a man who was very hard to like: self-aggrandizing and self-pitying. As a critic, he was mediocre; as a political columnist, engrossed in day-to-day squabbles; as a novelist, sentimental and imperialist' (p. 12). Wow! He really doesn't like Orwell. But overshadowing everything else was 'Orwell's role as an MI6 informant' (p. 59), his compiling and handing over a McCarthyite list to the Information Research Department (IRD), and, of course, the use that both the US and British secret states made of *Animal Farm* and *Nineteen Eighty-Four* during the Cold War. The problem is that, instead of looking at how Orwell's thinking developed over the years, at the impact that what he saw and experienced had on him, or at the influence that what he read and whom he discussed and argued with had on him, Reed is determined to identify the man as a McCarthyite sell-out through and through and to interpret his life and works as somehow leading up to, indeed culminating in, that final predetermined defining act of betrayal.

In effect, Reed is too focused on the so-called 'Orwell Cult' and has not got to grips adequately with the man's biography, the situations he faced and the choices he made. He does not successfully situate Orwell in the developing political context of his times. Certainly one of the great problems Orwell confronted was the impact that the Russian Revolution and its subsequent degeneration had on the left in Britain. The influence of Stalinism in Britain once the Popular Front turn had been adopted extended far beyond the Communist Party and Orwell was made aware of this, not least when he attempted to report what he had seen in Spain. As far as he was concerned, he had witnessed first-hand the communists betray the Spanish Revolution, smash the revolutionary left, murder, torture and defame their opponents and had only just escaped with his life himself. Back home, the only people prepared to listen to him were the anarchists, the Trotskyists and members of the Independent Labour Party, which he joined. Most of the British left was not interested. His account of his involvement in the Spanish Revolution, *Homage to Catalonia*, was rejected unseen by his publisher, Victor Gollancz, who had wholeheartedly embraced the 'Russian myth' at this time.

One cannot emphasise enough the importance of these months on Orwell's political trajectory. Orwell already had serious doubts regarding the development of Soviet Russia since the Revolution, but once he was back in Britain, he set about investigating the nature of the Stalin regime in more detail. What he found was that much of the left was celebrating a regime that far from building socialism was, in fact, presiding over famine, slave labour and terror on an unprecedented scale. Reed does not face up to the enormity of the crimes that the Stalinist regime committed in the name of socialism in the 1930s and 1940s, with much of the left, led by the communists, denying what was going on and at the same time slandering those exposing those crimes.

The hold of Stalinism in the 1930s was temporarily weakened by the conclusion of the Hitler-Stalin Pact in August 1939 with even Gollancz breaking with the Communist Party and welcoming Orwell back. With the Nazi invasion of the Soviet Union in June 1941, however, the situation was transformed, the Great Terror was soon forgotten and the mass murderer Joseph Stalin became our great ally 'Uncle Joe'. *Animal Farm* was written to try to counter this, and it is worth remembering that the Manor Farm regime that emerged under Napoleon in this book was not worse than the farms still controlled by capitalist farmers, but was just as bad – you could not tell the pigs from the men! Orwell was trying to counter the hold of the 'Russian myth' on the left. When he wrote the book the Soviet Union was still the ally of the British Empire and the United States; indeed, Stalin, Roosevelt and Churchill were busy carving the world up between them. Towards the end of *The Never End*, Reed does acknowledge that Orwell's 'disgust with Russia was more than justified', although *Animal Farm* was still 'a dose of poison' (p. 148). But this misses the point. He was at this time trying to fight the illusion that socialism was being built in the Soviet Union and that the Stalin regime was to be admired and even supported by the left. Reed would be much better served if he directed his scorn at those on the left who fell for Stalinism rather than at Orwell.

But what about the IRD list? Once again, towards the end of the book, Reed does admit that the Russian threat 'at the end of World War II was seemingly real', but goes on to ask: 'Did Orwell need to cooperate quite so enthusiastically?... Did he understand what he was doing?'(p. 148). He even argues at one point that Orwell would never have sold the film rights to *Animal Farm*, and he 'certainly wouldn't have given them to the military' (p. 135). Clearly Reed is conflicted. There are a number of factors that are relevant here. First, as far as Orwell was concerned, he was supporting a Labour government against the Soviet Union, a Labour government he certainly thought too timid and compromised but that was the best that was possible at the time. It was this government that established the Information Research Department which, as far as Orwell was concerned, was intended to counter the 'Soviet myth' and fight communist influence, propagating Labourite reformism as an alternative. His involvement with that organisation was clearly a serious mistake and the lists he handed over were absolutely shameful, but once again, it is worth remembering that, as far as he was concerned, all he was doing was advising against the employment by the IRD of people who were sympathetic to Stalinism. At this time, the Soviet Union was busy purging the so-called 'Titoites' across Eastern Europe, imprisoning hundreds of thousands of people and executing dozens of leading communists after rigged show trials. This was the context for Orwell's involvement with the IRD. This is not to justify his actions but to put them into context.

At the very same time, Orwell was actively defending civil liberties in Britain, including those of Communist Party members, people who would have cheerfully had him arrested, forced to confess, and executed if they had ever got into power. As for the use to which *Animal Farm* was put to attack the left generally, Orwell could not have made his objection to that clearer in a letter he wrote to the American Dwight Macdonald, a former Trotskyist who was moving towards anarchism : 'I meant the moral to be that revolutions only effect a radical improvement when the masses are alert and know how to chuck out their leaders as soon as the latter have done their job. … What I was trying to say was, "You can't have a revolution unless you make it for yourself ; there is no such thing as a benevolent dictatorship"'(Orwell 2013: 334).[1] Presumably, Reed would endorse these sentiments. Indeed, at one point he actually writes that 'I can't believe that he wanted *Animal Farm* to be a justification for unthinking conformity, which was something he feared and railed against' (p. 101). Only four pages later he describes the book as 'an educational missile aimed at any healthy impulse toward reform' (p. 105)! The problem is that while this was the use to which the book was put throughout the Cold War once Orwell was safely dead, Orwell cannot be blamed for that. Indeed, we can be sure that if he had lived longer he would only have endorsed the use made of the book by the British and US governments if his politics had dramatically changed, if he had completely abandoned the socialist politics that he still adhered to right up until his death.[2]

This brings us to what is potentially the most interesting part of Reed's book: his identification of Nikolai Kostomarov's story, 'Animal Riot', written in 1880, as a source for *Animal Farm*, something he first began investigating around 2013. As far as Reed is concerned, Orwell is inevitably guilty of plagiarism. The problem here is that he undermines his own case. He tells us that in 1934 Orwell was 'attending meetings of the Communist Party' where Kostomarov would have been discussed, that Kostomarov was 'commonly referenced in the books and scholarship of the day', that Orwell must have known about Kostomarov because he was 'one of the most significant Russian minds of the mid to late nineteenth century, a period that would have been the wellspring for Orwell's schooling and university education', that Orwell had 'at minimum rudimentary Russian', that he had heard about Kostomarov 'many, many times, too many to count' and that, crucially, he never denied being influenced by the 'Animal Riot' story (pp 22, 81, 91, 101). There is just so much wrong here that it is difficult to know where to begin, but it is worth noticing in passing that Kostomarov is not mentioned anywhere in Orwell's *Complete Works*. Nevertheless, this certainly requires further investigation and Reed has inspired this reader to take a closer look at Eileen Blair's friend Lydia Jackson, née Elisaveta Fen, née Lidiia Vitalievna Zhiburtovich, the translator of Chekhov, as a possible connection. Eileen, it is worth noticing, had, unlike George, actually been to university, St Hugh's College, Oxford, and had emerged with a degree in English. We shall see. The problem with Reed's identification of Kostomarov as a source for *Animal Farm*, however, is that he is not concerned to identify the influences on the man and his work, but rather sees it as another opportunity to discredit him. Taken as a whole, the book is primarily of interest as an example of the anti-Orwell Cult.

NOTES

[1] See the discussion in Newsinger (1999) pp 116-119

[2] It is impossible to resist pointing out that Reed missed one *Animal Farm* secret state connection when he notes that the introduction to the first US paperback edition of *Animal Farm* (1956) was written by Christopher Montague Woodhouse, the fifth Baron of Terrington (he only succeeded to the title in 1998), whom he describes as 'an Oxford professor and a conservative Parliamentary politician' (p. 52). He had, in fact, worked for the Special Operations Executive (the military arm of MI6) during the Second World War and for MI6 afterwards, playing an important role in Operation Boot, the US-British sponsored coup that overthrew the Mossadegh government in Iran in 1953

REFERENCES

Hitchens, Christopher (1993) Something about the poetry: Larkin and 'sensitivity', *New Left Review*, Vol. 200, July-August

Newsinger, John (1993a) Dead poet: The Larkin letters, *Race and Class*, Vol. 34, No. 4 April

Newsinger, John (1993b) An episode in the Larkin wars, *New Left Review*, Vol. 202, November-December

Newsinger, John (1999) *Orwell's Politics*, Basingstoke: Macmillan

Orwell, George (2013) *A Life in Letters*, Davison, Peter (ed.) New York: Penguin

John Newsinger,
Bath Spa University

Polymath: The Life and Professions of Dr Alex Comfort, Author of *The Joy of Sex*

Eric Laursen

AK Press, Chico/Edinburgh, 2023 pp 760

ISBN: 9781849354967

Eric Laursen's *The Duty to Stand Aside* (AK Press) in which he examines with great panache the wartime quarrel between George Orwell and Alex Comfort, is one of my favourite texts in the vast Orwellian canon. The text throws light on a fascinating character usually marginalised in the conventional biographies and, in the process, explores a number of crucially important issues relating to pacifism, anarchism, war-fighting, freedom of expression, the value of friendship – and the cancer of secrecy.[1]

Laursen has now followed up that 2018 study with a 700-plus-page, massively researched, pioneering biography, *Polymath: The Life and Professions of Alex Comfort* (2023), exploring – in impressive detail – the life and writings of one of the most remarkable (yet undervalued) intellectuals of the second half of the twentieth century.

For Comfort was distinguished in so many areas: as a poet, novelist, dramatist, television script writer, biologist, sexologist, gerontologist, medical doctor, translator from the French and Sanskrit, travel writer, sociologist, cultural critic, political theorist and peace activist, anarchist and expert on mollusks. But most famously he was the author of the international bestselling *The Joy of Sex*, which has moved more than twelve million copies (to date) in a host of languages since it appeared in 1972. As Laursen explains (pp 1-2):

> Almost a dozen years earlier, he had experienced a midlife sexual reawakening when he commenced an affair with a family friend. They turned her London flat into the scene of a long course in sexual experiment, complete with Polaroid photographs, a detailed notebook and extensive delving into lovemaking texts from ancient India, Japan and Renaissance Italy. Distressed by the raft of dubious sex primers hitting the market in the late '60s … Comfort decided to write his own.

The biography is impressive in covering all of Comfort's vast oeuvre, his diverse professional activities, his eclectic intellectual interests and his personal life (with a tumultuous second marriage) in astonishing depth. Comfort's relationship with Orwell (the subject of this review) forms just a small part. Yet it gives an indication of how the complex personal, political, cultural and intellectual contexts are covered so comprehensively and critically throughout. And Laursen has clearly enjoyed delving into the archives: at University College London, the Kinsey Institute for Research in Sex, Gender and Reproduction, the Harry Ransom Center at the University of Texas, the University of Bradford and Bishopsgate Library, London.

NONCOMFORMISM OF PARENTS 'AT THE ROOT OF PACIFISM'
Comfort (1920-2000) grew up in Barnet, Hertfordshire, and Laursen sees the roots of his pacifism in the middle class, Nonconformism of his parents. But his life was primarily shaped by his brilliant and formidable mother, Elizabeth, who came from a working class London family, a born teacher 'who took a dogmatic and pedagogical approach to everything and everyone' (p. 13). 'Under Elizabeth's tutelage, Alex spoke French almost from birth' (p. 14). In 1934, he wins a scholarship in classics to Highgate 'one of the dozen or so best English public or independent schools but distinctly less prestigious than the "posh" institutions, notably Eton and Harrow, that trained well-born boys to be gentlemen' (p. 25). But while at home on a break in March 1935, a chemistry experiment goes disastrously wrong and in an explosion he loses three fingers of his left hand. 'The accident – sudden, shocking, agonizing – changed Alex's life forever. His absorption in learning and conspicuous evangelicalism already set him apart from many of the other boys at Highgate. Now, the difference was physical as well' (p. 29).

While at Cambridge, where he sits papers in Physiology, Anatomy, Biochemistry, Pathology and Zoology (and where his tutor is A.S.F. Gow, Orwell's classics tutor at Eton), he has his first novel, *No Such Liberty*, published by Chapman & Hall. Orwell's first contact with Comfort now comes with his review of *No Such Liberty*, in *Adelphi*, in October 1941. In the novel, a young German couple, pathologist Dr Helmut Breitz who is a Christian pacifist, and his wife, Anna, flee the Nazis to England. But as a pacifist, Breitz is classified as a class B alien and the couple are placed in internment camps where their child suffers neglect and undernourishment before dying. Comfort is highlighting the similarities between the two countries at a time of war. But as England faced imminent invasion by the Nazis, Orwell was being outspoken in his support for the war effort and in his denunciations of pacifists. So in his review, Orwell argues that Comfort is practising 'a high-brow variant of British hypocrisy. The sufferings of his German doctor in a so-called democratic country are so terrible as to wipe out every shred of moral justification for the struggle against Fascism.' Orwell concludes: 'Objectively the pacifist is pro-Nazi' (p. 70).

Laursen clearly admires both Comfort (he calls him perhaps over-intimately Alex throughout) and Orwell. But this does not stop him from criticising them when he feels necessary. Here, he is rightly critical of Orwell's intemperate response:

> While the main character of *No Such Liberty* is a pacifist, as was the author, the novel itself is not; it ends with no clear path forward for Breitz or for anyone concerned with the impact the war was having on civilized life. And while it spotlights the government's poor treatment of refugees, it does not imply any moral equivalence between Britain and Germany; it only points up abuses that war makes inevitable and warns against the possibility that Britain could resort to conduct like the Nazis. Nor does it make any argument against resisting Nazism, especially for people living under it (ibid).

ORWELL ATTACKS ANTI-WAR CAMPAIGNERS FOR 'DEFEATISM'

Orwell's interest in Comfort as a writer is further sparked when he hears his poem 'The Atoll of the Mind' read by Herbert Read during his talk on 'The New Romantic School' on the BBC's Indian Service (p. 85). But then, in the summer of 1941, the journal *NOW*, being edited by George Woodcock, a Canadian conscientious objector, includes pieces by eccentric anti-war campaigner Hugh Ross Williamson and the antisemitic Duke of Bedford. An angry Orwell launches all-out attack on 'defeatism' and again accuses British pacifists of forming an alliance with the enemy.

> 'More ominously,' Orwell wrote: 'I do seem to notice a tendency in intellectuals, especially the younger ones, to come to terms with Fascism, and it is a thing to keep one's eye on. … If the Germans got to England … I think I could make out at least a preliminary list of the people who would go over' (p. 88).

This draws an equally furious response from Comfort, Woodcock and Derek Savage, a Christian poet. According to Comfort: 'Hitler's greatest and irretrievable victory over here was when he persuaded the English people that the only way to lick Fascism was to imitate it.' Men like Orwell who could have helped preserve civilised values 'are calling us Fascists and presumably dancing around the ruins of Munster Cathedral. We prefer not to join them'. Orwell hits back: 'The idea that you can somehow remain aloof from and superior to the struggle while living on food which British soldiers have to risk their lives to bring you, is a bourgeois illusion bred of money and security' (ibid). Laursen again critiques Orwell's response as 'a bit hysterical':

> None of the people he was attacking are known to have secretly helped the Nazis during the war. ... But his complete lack of sympathy with pacifism as such made it impossible for Orwell to understand what its adherents expected to accomplish by speaking against the war. – critiquing the treatment of refugees and enemy aliens, the government's abandonment of its prewar commitment to spare civilians in its bombing campaigns, its use of blockades that starved whole populations and its use of hate speech to turn enemy nations into pariahs (p. 89).

In April 1943, after Comfort has just passed the first of two examinations for his Bachelor of Medicine degree, his first letter to *Tribune* putting the pacifist case is published. Two months later his 'Letter to an American Visitor', a 15-stanza poem. under the pseudonym Obadiah Hornbrooke, appears (p. 107):

BOOK REVIEW

> Verse after verse ridiculed Churchill's stirring speeches as 'the dim productions of his bulldog brain', reviled the church's willingness to preach 'that bombs [were] Christian when the English drop[ped] them' and insinuated that Britain's literary giants were willing to turn out propaganda in exchange for avoiding military service.

Laursen here cleverly focuses on what Comfort leaves out: there is a personal attack on the poet Louis MacNeice, who had joined the BBC at about the same time as Orwell to produce cultural programmes, but none on Orwell nor on his friends Herbert Read and George Woodcock who are by now participating in Orwell's BBC radio programmes. But Laursen also criticises Comfort for coming 'disturbingly close to dismissing the unprecedented atrocities Germany was committing and impugning the motives of many artists and writers who were working hard and without much reward to defeat fascism' (ibid).

Two weeks later on 18 June, Orwell's response, a Byronic satire 'As One Non-Combatant to Another (A Letter to 'Obadiah Hornbrooke'), is published. It ends on a witty note urging Comfort not to end up a saintly pacifist: 'So my last word would be: Come off that cloud/Unship those wings that hardly dared to flitter,/And spout your halo for a pint of bitter' (p. 109).

HOW FRIENDSHIP DEVELOPS BETWEEN THE TWO MEN

After sparring poetically against each other in public, a friendly correspondence develops between the two men. In one letter, Comfort concedes that John Middleton Murry, editing *Peace News* for the pacifist Peace Pledge Union, erred in arguing that violence is wrong and immoral and that the conflict with Germany would destabilise the British Empire. Soon afterwards Orwell agrees to submit an article to Comfort's journal *New Road*: a cut-down version of his short memoir 'Looking Back on the Spanish Civil War' will appear in the first 1943 edition. And Orwell writes congratulating Comfort on the quality of the writing in his *Tribune* poem.

Then, on his first day at *Tribune* as literary editor in November 1943, after quitting the BBC, Orwell writes letters of invitation to the poets, T.S. Eliot and Henry Treece while to Comfort he says: 'I should like very much if you could do another satirical poem' (p. 117). Comfort's response, 'The Little Apocalypse of Obadiah Hornbrooke', satirising wartime propaganda, is published on 30 June. When this provokes furious letters from readers, Orwell answers them saying that while he did not agree with Hornbrooke, there were lines the editors would not cross: 'We wouldn't print an article in praise of antisemitism, for instance. But granted the necessary minimum of agreement, literary merit is the only thing that matters.' He goes further in defending Comfort: '… there is quite a strong case for saying that British imperialism is actually worse than Nazism' (p. 118).

Laursen throughout highlights the development of Comfort's ideas in forensic detail. In 'Art and Social Responsibility', for Woodcock's *Now*, he begins searching in psychoanalysis for an understanding of the 'madness' of war. The war was not between classes but between individuals and society. 'The goal must be to secede from society and the State and in their place form communities of free individuals practising mutual aid.' But again Laursen is on hand to offer pointed criticism: 'The writing is often clumsy, his terms are not always well defined and he repeats himself and bludgeons home point after point' (p. 121). Comparing conditions among Dachau inmates to anarchism and ascribing to prisoners the power to create in the face of oncoming starvation and murder was about as unthinking, not to mention insensitive a statement as a writer could make who argued for 'boundless responsibility for the voiceless' (ibid).

When in December 1944, Special Branch raids the offices of the anarchist Freedom Press on a warrant issued under Defence Regulation 39a which made it an offence to 'endeavour to cause disaffection amongst persons engaged … in his Majesty's Service', Orwell is appalled. The homes of prominent anarchists are also raided while copies *of War Commentary*, *Peace News* and *NOW* are seized. The police were responding to a manifesto in *War Commentary* calling on armed services to practise mass disobedience as soon as the war was over. Orwell even becomes vice-chair of the

Freedom Press Defence Committee (the only post he ever accepts) with Herbert Read chair and George Woodcock secretary (p. 142). Letters of protest are sent to *Tribune* and *New Statesman and Nation* signed by Orwell, Eliot, Forster, Spender, Osbert Sitwell, Bertrand Russell, Julian Symons and Dylan Thomas. Comfort is cautious and concerned that the response could be 'too militant' (p. 143).

In the end, of the four core members of the Freedom collective who are charged, Marie Louise Berneri, wife of Vernon Richards, is acquitted since under English law a wife could not conspire with her husband while the other three are given comparatively light sentences of nine months' imprisonment in Wormwood Scrubs.

Comfort and Orwell meet in person for the first and only time in 1945, just after the Freedom Press trial and the publication of *Animal Farm,* at a pub in Bermondsey. What is actually said at the meeting is open to dispute. In a chapter in a collection of essays on *Nineteen Eighty-Four*, edited by Peter Stansky in 1983, Comfort writes that 'Orwell told me about the new novel he was working on *Nineteen Eighty-Four*, which I took to be a political statement against dictatorship. His reply was astonishing – that it was, but that the model in his mind was also that of the neurotic's internal "thought police", with Big Brother as the superego' (p. 196). Laursen is actually at fault for not querying this extraordinary quotation. After all, Orwell could hardly have been talking about *Nineteen Eighty-Four* in 1945. Its original working title was *Last Man in Europe* and this was only changed much later close to publication. Orwell's talk about neurosis and the superego is untypical – but it might suggest the influence of his first wife, Eileen O'Shaughnessy, who had studied educational psychology at University College London before meeting Orwell in 1935. Or was Comfort merely projecting his own ideas on to Orwell?

The two men next join their pacifist/anarchist colleagues in condemning the nuclear bombing of Hiroshima and Nagasaki, in August 1945. In an article in *War Commentary*, just two weeks later, Comfort writes: 'We have just witnessed an act of criminal lunacy which must be without parallel in recorded history. A city of 300,000 people [Hiroshima] has been suddenly and deliberately obliterated and its inhabitants murdered by the English and American governments' (p. 146). Laursen is again on hand to offer both criticism and praise: ascribing the bombing to the English as well as the American governments was erroneous. 'But Alex was not wrong in arguing that the nuclear attacks were a logical extension of the Allied bombing campaign and more than two decades of state infatuation with aerial warfare' (ibid).

Orwell, writing in *Tribune* in October, is less focused on actual events – he concentrates rather on the effect on the state itself.

Without quite saying so, he indicates that three empires will come to dominate a new permanent state of 'cold war': Western Europe and United States, the Soviet Union and East Asia dominated by China. As Laursen comments, such ideas foreshadow 'the dystopia he was already turning into compelling fiction in the manuscript of *Nineteen Eighty-Four*' (p. 147).

COMFORT AND THE 'LITTLE LIST' OF CRYPTO-COMMUNISTS

Laursen leaves covering one of the most controversial aspects of the Orwell/Comfort relationship somewhat awkwardly until page 623 – in the Conclusion and under a subheading 'Afterlife'. This is Orwell's decision to include Comfort in the 'little list' of 38 crypto-communists he sends to the government's secret propaganda unit, the Information Research Department, in 1949. On Comfort's potential collaboration with communists, he writes: 'Potential only. Is pacifist-anarchist. Main emphasis anti-British. Subjectively pro-German during war, appears temperamentally pro-totalitarian. Not morally courageous. Has a crippled hand. Very talented.'

To imply that Comfort was on the Germans' side – this even though he never wrote a sympathetic word about Hitler's regime, is outrageous – all the more so since at the time Orwell compiled the list they were collaborating on the Freedom Defence Committee. Significantly, fellow anarchist George Woodcock and Herbert Read do not appear on the list. Laursen suggests that, had he known, Comfort would have been taken aback. 'I counted Orwell as a friend,' Comfort wrote in 1983. Moreover, his son, Nick, who is quoted throughout the text, remembers that his father always spoke of Orwell with great respect and didn't recall him ever knowing that Orwell had included him on the list, a full copy of which only surfaced in 2003 (p. 625)

Laursen is ultimately critical, rightly so I feel: 'While Orwell's carelessly assembled memo was not a blacklist – he wasn't seeking to get anyone fired – it brought Alex and dozens of others to the attention of the state intelligence apparatus that might abuse that information. … The fact that Alex never knew Orwell had named him and thus never had a chance to answer back to the distorted mini-portrait Orwell painted is one of the minor but telling injustices of the Cold War era' (p. 627).

NOTE

[1] See Keeble, Richard Lance (2021) Throwing light on the crucial quarrel with Comfort, Keeble, Richard Lance, *Orwell's Moustache*, Bury St Edmunds: Abramis pp 93-101

Richard Lance Keeble,
University of Lincoln

George Orwell: The Ethics of Equality

Peter Brian Barry

Oxford: Oxford University Press pp 280

ISBN: 9780197627402 (hbk)

BOOK REVIEW

In an interview published in this issue of *George Orwell Studies*, D.J. Taylor describes the durability of Orwell's legacy and how his reputation is rivalled by few other authors. Truly, Orwell's ideas have reached a level of cultural permeation that shadows many of the thought-leaders alive in his time and even outshines many in our own time. Such is the underlying, if unacknowledged, premise of Peter Brian Barry's *George Orwell: The Ethics of Equality*. After all, if 'Orwellian' is a common adjective and Orwell retains a status amongst the great literary saints (if sometimes an ambivalent one), why should he not *also* be a philosopher? And what stops us from considering his most forceful ideas – detailed in chapters on human decency, free will and rhetorical power – as the foundation of an ethics? This question – about the existence of an Orwellian philosophy or ethics – lies at the centre of this book. In its chapters, each discussing various strands of Orwell's ethical thought, Barry outlines the 'ethical principles and concepts that pervade Orwell's work consistently and ground some of his better-known positions and pronouncements' (p. x).

The project, as Barry admits, is inherently counterintuitive for a few reasons. For one, Orwell was no self-branded philosopher. He was not, like H.G. Wells, interested in being an academic nor even in engaging with much philosophical thought. In fact, Barry correctly remarks that Orwell was 'at best indifferent to academic and abstract philosophy if not outright hostile to it' (p. x). That is not the only challenge to an Orwellian ethics, Barry admits; another challenge posed by the study is the perennial risk in any effort to articulate the *oeuvre* of a writer in terms of a series of consistent philosophical principles. At times, Orwell shifts in and out of sub-categories, just as he does in Barry's chapters on egalitarianism and libertarianism.

Yet, by taking these reasonable hesitations into consideration, Barry provides compelling insights into Orwell's writings as he uses philosophy to 'identify and articulate those ethical principles and concepts' that become so crucial in Orwell's work (p. 247). If

'Orwellian' can be a byword for tyranny, it might also be applied to a school of thought, even if that philosophy is that of the man who was Orwell. Thus, upon concluding, the reader finds the question 'Is Orwell a philosopher?' both unanswered and made irrelevant. Amidst books highlighting the power of Orwell's legacy, including John Rodden's *Becoming George Orwell* and Dorian Lynskey's *The Ministry of Truth*, Barry is right to consider Orwell's thought within the realm of the philosophical. By juxtaposing Orwell's thought to debates in philosophy, incorporating works by Socrates, Rousseau, Rawls and the Frankfurt School, we come to new versions of Orwell and even the nature of what it is to be 'Orwellian'. Among these new versions of Orwell Barry includes in *The Ethics of Equality* are Orwell as relational egalitarian (p. 187) and Orwell as threshold deontologist (p. 30).

Aside from the Introduction, which frames Orwell's overt position vis-à-vis philosophy (not much of one, as Barry acknowledges), the remaining chapters take up various strands of Orwell's thought in light of that very philosophy. This includes chapters on his attitudes on free will, moral responsibility, moral psychology, decency, egalitarianism, libertarianism and socialism.

So what is an Orwellian ethics? One real surprise from this book is that, according to Barry, many Orwell fans may begin their search for his ethics in the wrong place: decency. Orwellian decency is, perhaps, one of the most evocative of his concepts and even the one most suggestive of a philosophical position. Decency is appraised in detail by a range of Orwellian critics including Peter Davison, George Woodcock and John Rodden. Yet, as Barry notes, Orwell's use of 'decency' is often amorphous, undefinable and even sentimental at times. This is highlighted in the chapter 'Orwellian Decency', where the reader finds that 'Orwellian decency, whatever it is, is not a moral virtue' (p. 129). Of course, Barry does not deny the concept its importance to Orwell's thought but, instead, suggests that decency 'cannot do the job he wants it to do' (p. 129). Of course, there is the obvious fact, even if Orwell's vision of the 'decent man' is meant to convey something akin to a universal good, that his varied descriptions of decency across the course of his career suggest the difficulty in finding any certainty there. Barry also claims that 'forms of … decency emerge only from within a social practice of morality' (p. 133), thus emphasising the contextual and subjective nature of the concept.

But if decency cannot hold the status of an ethics, Barry's comparison of Orwell's decency to John Rawls's vision of a decent society is still provocative. For example, when analysing the passage from *Keep the Aspidistra Flying* where Gordon Comstock rails against his indecent clothing, Barry suggests that while the passage may propose decency as a stand-in for a certain 'bourgeois morality', a more nuanced reading may suggest that Comstock is prefiguring the Rawlsian notion that a decent society must necessarily foster the kind of self-respect Comstock seeks, but otherwise lacks. Certainly, Orwell would have agreed that 'even mere decency is unlikely without self-respect' (p. 140). But, as Barry's critique of decency as a moral virtue suggests, any disambiguation of bourgeois moralism from a concern with self-respect is perhaps impossible; after all, what is a self-respect but the affirmation of some version of contextually defined moralism, bourgeois or otherwise? And from what other foundation was Orwell to form a notion of self-respect but from his own position, both in and out of the bourgeois networks he so often criticised?

In his chapter 'George Orwell: The Age's Advocate', Barry reads against the vision of Orwell as 'an adversary, not an advocate' by presenting facets of philosophy that may better suggest Orwell's positive message. Barry frames Orwell against consequentialists like Bentham and Mill, who see the good located in the greatest happiness for the greatest number. But he also sees Orwell arguing in favour of an anti-Benthamite view of good action, which takes into account the suffering of the few more concretely than would consequentialism. Thus, we find Orwell's anti-consequentialism – his refusal to abide by the principles of Bentham and others – not only in his essays critiquing Hitler but also, perhaps unexpectedly, in his critiques of Gandhi, whose saintliness he considered 'morally dubious because of its consequentialist and anti-humanist demand that we abandon human attachments' (p. 52).

Orwell the man often failed to grapple effectively with the inherent and human inconsistencies between thought and action. But, as Barry reminds us, these very human failures may only better help define Orwell's moral position. While noting Orwell's dismissive attitudes towards women as critiqued by feminist scholars such as Daphne Patai, Barry acknowledges that those sexist attitudes 'do not reconcile well with a relational egalitarianism that prides living together as equals', which was key to Orwell's thought (p. 186). He continues: '[I]f Orwell's sexism disappoints us, it is surely because he is otherwise well regarded as a relational egalitarian. We expect better from him because he is responsive to moral reasons for abandoning other morally dubious beliefs and practices of his day' (ibid). That Orwell's laudable goals are not always reflected in his actions – as in his distinctly unpleasant writings (at times) about homosexuality, Jews or women – is hardly a refutation of Orwellian thought, Barry writes, but an emphasis on the limits of its application.

BOOK REVIEW

Barry ends the book focusing on liberty and egalitarianism. In both instances, as with decency, he affirms these approaches as essential to Orwell's view of a good society while also adding nuance to the positions. For instance, in his chapter on Orwell's libertarianism, he suggests that 'the case for thinking that Orwell is well-understood as a left-libertarian is underdetermined' (p. 216). But it is this very philosophical ambivalence, Barry suggests, that can lead to clarification of many of Orwell's political positions. For example, readers will find great value in his argument in the chapter on democratic socialism, which builds from Orwell's ambivalence to any purist leftist libertarianism to argue that Orwell's 'case for democratic Socialism … flows from his egalitarianism and *not* from a commitment to a stringent right of self-ownership' (p. 217).

Megan Faragher,
Wright State University,
Dayton,
Ohio

REVIEW ESSAY

Wifedom: Fundamentally Flawed

RICHARD LANCE KEEBLE

Anna Funder's life of Eileen O'Shaughnessy, the first wife of George Orwell, follows in the tradition of studies of the wives and lovers of famous artists who have been largely ignored in the conventional biographies. These include Brenda Maddox's *Nora: A Biography of Nora Joyce* (1988), Claire Tomalin's *The Invisible Woman: The Story of Nelly Ternan and Charles Dickens* (1990), Stacy Schiff's *Vera (Mrs Vladimir Nabokov)* (1999), Sally Cline's *Zelda Fitzgerald* (2003), Suzanne Fagence Cooper's *The Passionate Lives of Effie Gray, Ruskin and Millais* (2010), Cate Haste's *The Passionate Spirit: The Life of Alma Mahler* (2019). And, in 2020, of special interest to Orwellians came Sylvia Topp's pathbreaking biography of Eileen.

In *Wifedom* (London: Viking, 2023), Anna Funder mixes stern critique of Orwell with some passing comments of clear admiration. For instance, she writes (p. 85): 'His desire to expose hidden people from under society's hypocrisies that keep us blind to them is so admirable, and so exciting. The project of good writing (to reveal to us the world we thought we knew) is perfectly combined with a political project (to reveal the world we thought we knew so we can change it).' Of *Homage to Catalonia*, she says: 'I've loved this book since I was a teen' (p. 97)

Her major critique is that Orwell consistently devalues, ignores and trivialises the role of women – and that of his first wife in particular. She suggests that while Orwell went down-and-out to investigate the poor 'he might have gone "down and in" to investigate the living conditions of women and wives, even his own' (p. 85). When women can't be left out altogether, 'they are doubted, trivialized or reduced to footnotes in 8-point font' (p. 60).

Funder is rightly highly critical of Orwell's many affairs behind Eileen's back – such as with Una Marson, and Hetta Crouse while he was working at the BBC (1941-1943); he even attempted to have a sexual affair with Eileen's friend Lydia Jackson (Elisaveta Fen). 'Going for your wife's close friend is an act calculated to undermine your wife. That way she will be all the more totally alone, and so all the more yours' (p. 217). Lydia's role in the affair is ambivalent but Funder settles on describing her as 'an unwilling accomplice' (p. 218). On Orwell's 'open marriage', she writes (p. 273):

> Because the biographers would like to believe that Eileen and Orwell agreed to an open marriage, they must try to find evidence of Eileen taking lovers. But aside from [Georges] Kopp's love for her (and no one knows if they slept together) there are none. I find myself wishing that there were, but there's only a friend of her brother who admired her, and vague, single-source rumours of someone high up at the BBC.

But no sources are provided for the 'rumours of someone high up at the BBC'. Moreover, her suggestions that Orwell made love to Celia Kirwan 'Burma-sergeant fashion' in 1945 – and that she later travelled to Barnhill, the farmhouse on the remote Scottish island of Jura where Orwell composed *Nineteen Eighty-Four*, to see him – have appalled members of Kirwan's family and corrections are to be included in a revised edition. According to Quentin Kopp, chair of The Orwell Society and son of Orwell's commander in Spain, Funder has 'imposed a modern feminist view on a marriage of 80 years ago. She has also decided to attack Orwell, for whatever reasons, in a book which is destructive of him and his reputation' (Brooks 2023).

Funder highlights the unpaid, unrecognised work Eileen does for Orwell throughout their relationship. For instance, immediately after their marriage in 1936 (pp 75-76) while Orwell writes and writes 'Eileen deals with the "dreadful" resident Aunt (there for *two months*!), the chickens, the goat and the visitors. She makes thwarted attempts to take a (working) break with her brother, who needs her help editing his scientific papers' (italics in the original).

Orwell's behaviour towards women is placed within a broader context (p. 50): 'Every society in the world is built on the unpaid or underpaid work of women. If it had to be paid for it would cost, apparently, US$10.9 trillion. But to pay for it would be to redistribute wealth and power in a way that might defund and de-fang patriarchy.' She adds (p. 221): 'Patriarchy *is* the doublethink that allowed an apparently "decent" man to behave badly to women, in the same way as colonialism and racism are systems that allow apparently "decent" people to do unspeakable things to other people.'

Wifedom mixes memoir, confessional, imagined scenes from Eileen's life often incorporating verbatim reproductions of her letters to friend Norah Myles (first published in 2006) and those to family members included in Peter Davison's *A Life in Letters* (2013 [2010]) – and largely damning critiques of the seven leading

Orwellian biogs (all written by men). Sylvia Topp's indispensable biography of Eileen is largely ignored and only mentioned in the notes.

Much is drawn from the testimony of Eileen's friend Lydia Jackson, her *A Russian's England* and her essay on Eileen. At one point Funder visits various sites where Orwell either fought or visited during the Spanish Civil War in 1937 with 'a dozen people with an interest in Orwell' (presumably members of The Orwell Society) along with Richard Blair, Orwell and Eileen's adopted son, and Quentin Kopp (pp 112-113). Later she travels to Barnhill, the farmhouse on the remote Scottish island of Jura where Orwell composed *Nineteen Eighty-Four*. In these ways the personal blends in with the biographical narrative.

SERIOUS PROBLEMATICS

Yet there are serious problematics about the text. Early on she quotes from Orwell's last notebook (p. 11):

> There were two great facts about women which … you could only learn by getting married & which flatly contradicted the picture of themselves that women had managed to impose upon the world. One was their incorrigible dirtiness and untidiness. The other was their terrible, devouring sexuality. … Within any marriage or regular love affair, he suspected that it was always the woman who was the sexually insistent partner. In his experience women were quite insatiable, & never seemed fatigued by no matter how much love-making … In any marriage of more than a year or two's standing, intercourse was thought of as a duty, a service owned by the man to the woman. And he suspected that in every marriage the struggle was always the same – the man trying to escape from sexual intercourse, to do it only when he felt like it (or with other women), the woman demanding it more & more, & more & more consciously despising her husband for his lack of virility.

She adds (p. 12): 'Orwell only ever lived with one wife. These comments refer to Eileen.' But do they?

Funder goes through the biographies and examines their treatment of this text (pp 12-13): 'There seemed to be no way for the biographers to deal with this anti-woman, anti-wife, anti-sex rant other than by leaving it out, sympathizing with the impulse, trivializing it as a "mood", denying it as "fiction" or blaming the woman herself.' Yet there is always a danger to conflate Orwell the man with Orwell the imaginative writer. As the French novelist and literary theorist, Anne F. Garréta, writes (1996: 212-213):

RICHARD LANCE KEEBLE

I would like to read Proust's contention that "a book is the product of an I different from the one we manifest in our habits, in society, in our vices" as an index of a certain dissembling afforded by literature. The empirical self and the writing (or reading) self are not identical; fiction is the realm where identities, far from being reinforced may be displaced.

In his last writings, Orwell is clearly keen to explore questions relating to authorial 'voice'. His memoir of his years at St Cyprian's prep school, 'Such, Such Were the Joys', deliberately mixes memoir and fiction. Even in his last notebook, he devotes a sizeable section to examining the case 'for & against novels in the first person' (*CWGO* XX: 205). In other words, it is too simplistic to suggest that the appalling 'sexist rant' in the last notebook is Orwell's own (rather than imagined) voice. Interestingly, Funder explores this issue of authenticity in a chapter titled 'Mind the gap' and concludes appropriately: '… a person is not their work, just where it came from' (p. 224).

CRITIQUE OF SEVEN (MALE) BIOGRAPHERS

Another serious problem is that Funder tends to lump all the seven biographers (named only in the notes) together in her criticisms. Typically, she writes (p. 20): 'Orwell's biographers are seven men looking at a man. Each of them is brilliant and each tells a slightly different story – slanted now towards heroism and forgiveness, now towards "dark recesses" of unnamed complexity. But all of them minimize the importance of the women in Orwell's life. In the end, the biographers started to seem like fictions of omissions.' Yet the index of Jeffrey Meyers biography (2000: 376) has 45 entries under the sub-heading 'relationships with women' with separate sections for Mabel Fierz, Inez Holden, Lydia Jackson, Eleanor Jaques, Sally Jerome, Celia Paget, Anne Popham, Brenda Salkeld, Stevie Smith, Susan Watson and Kay Welton.

From the Orwell biographers, she suggests (p. 58): 'You would not learn that his mother, Ida, was a Fabian socialist and suffragette, educated in England.' But Bowker (2003: 16) says of Ida and her sister Nellie that they: '… attended Suffragette meetings and moved in Fabian circles, hobnobbing with writers such as Wells, Chesterton and E. Nesbit (author of not just *The Railway Children* and the *Would-be Gods*, but also *The Ballads and Lyrics of Socialism*), and radicals such as Conrad Noel, the famous vicar of Thaxted who flew the red flag from his church tower, and was at that time Nellie's local curate in Paddington, a pioneer of Christian socialism who spent his spare time in London lodging houses among the down-and-outs'.

Funder says the biographers do not make the link between Nellie and important writers and thinkers such as Chesterton, Wells and E. Nesbit but we have seen Bowker, for one, making these links.

She is right to suggest that Orwell never admitted to his appalling attempted rape of his childhood friend Jacintha Buddicom (though Funder does not for some reason supply the family name) but equally Jacintha never mentions it in her memoir of her years of friendship with Eric Blair (as she knew him). Both probably felt embarrassment and shame about the incident and kept it secret.

HOW WOMEN, IN FACT, FEATURE IN THE WRITINGS ON THE PLIGHT OF THE POOR

Orwell's trip to the north of England in 1936 to examine the plight of the poor, unemployed and miners – his researches later published as *The Road to Wigan Pier* (1937), which Funder describes as 'wonderful' (p. 64) – is given only a passing mention. Significantly feminist critic Beatrix Campbell compares Orwell's celebration of the miners' manly labour with his denigration of the work of women: 'Women do not appear as protagonists in Orwell's working class' (1984: 129). Deirdre Beddoe likewise argues that Orwell concentrated on mining as a largely male preserve so ignoring the cotton industry 'where women predominated' (Beddoe 1984: 148).

Ben Clarke draws from *Caliban Boswelling*, the unpublished autobiography of Jack Hilton, the working class writer to whom Orwell corresponded before heading north, to suggest that Orwell concentrated on the mines after originally planning to visit the mill town of Rochdale. '*Caliban Boswelling* suggests that this decision was influenced by some of his working-class contacts [such as Hilton], who discouraged him from concentrating on mills despite his initial intentions' (Clarke 2016).

And yet women *do* feature in the detailed diary he wrote while on the trip (Keeble 2023). In Sheffield, he has a long conversation with Mrs Searle (judging by the length of his profile of her) and comments: 'I was surprised by Mrs S.'s grasp of the economic situation and also of abstract ideas' (*CEJL* 1: 220). On 16 March 1936, Orwell writes colourfully of the meeting he attends the previous night at a packed Barnsley Public Hall addressed by the fascist leader Oswald Mosley. A number of protestors are violently thrown out by some of the 100 Blackshirts on duty and Orwell later notes that a woman ejected 'was hit on the head with a trumpet and was a day in hospital' (ibid: 233).

On 18 March, he makes a special mention of a very old Lancashire woman 'who in her day has worked down the pit, dragging tubs of coal with a harness and chain. She is 83, so I suppose this would be in the seventies' (ibid: 234). When he attends a social evening

REVIEW ESSAY

RICHARD LANCE KEEBLE

organised by the National Union of Mine Workers to raise money for the defence fund of Ernst Thaelmann, chairman of the German Communist Party who had been arrested in 1933, he notices that most of the 200 people present are women. And on 22 March, he reports on a 'disappointing' communist meeting in Wigan Market Place though 'the usual handful of women a little more animated than the men – I suppose because no woman would go to a political meeting unless exceptionally interested in politics' (ibid: 241).

Orwell even shows himself sensitive to gender politics in the home and beyond. On 5 March, he records the controversy he causes when he helps Mrs Searle with the washing up (ibid: 222). The two men of the house disapprove. Orwell continues: 'Mrs S. seemed doubtful. She said that in the North working class men never offered any courtesies to women (women are allowed to do all the house-work unaided even when the man is unemployed and it is always the man who sits on the comfortable chair) and she took these things for granted but did not see why it should not be changed.' Men, she says, would lose their manhood if they stooped to doing any housework (except carpentering and gardening).

The most celebrated representation of a woman in *The Road to Wigan Pier* comes when he leaves Wigan by train. He writes:

> At the back of one of the houses a young woman was kneeling on the stones, poking a stick up the leaden waste-pipe which ran from the sink inside and which I suppose was blocked. I had time to see everything about her – her sacking apron, her clumsy clogs, her arms reddened by the cold. She looked up as the train passed, and I was almost near enough to catch her eye. She had a round pale face, the usual exhausted face of the slum girl who is twenty-five and looks forty, thanks to miscarriages and drudgery, and it wore, for the second in which I saw it, the most desolate, hopeless expression I have ever seen (1980 [1937]: 131).

Interestingly, the account differs in the diary. Rather than seeing the woman from a train, Orwell, on 15 February 1936, records seeing her while on a walking tour with NUMW officials collecting facts about housing conditions: 'At the moment she looked up and caught my eye and her expression was as desolate as I have ever seen; it struck me that she was thinking just the same thing as I was' (*CEJL* I: 2013). So why did Orwell make this change? According to biographer Bernard Crick, Orwell transformed the 'flat' account in the diary into literature, showing his 'growing skill as a writer, his ability to use, not to be dominated by his material, to keep the essentials in mind, not to lose the wood for the trees' (1980: 287). '… the train leaving Wigan is itself a symbol of the writer's almost desperate pain at being merely an observer, a member of another class who, having done his contracted task, is carried off remorselessly and mechanically simply to write about "what can be done"' (ibid).

Funder carries this reference to the woman ground down by domestic work to a footnote (p. 407) and adds: 'This insight, however, did not change the way he lived with Eileen, who did all the domestic work' (p. 408)

According to Funder, no biographer quotes Lydia saying she thought Blair unattractive and that Eileen deserved someone better. But, again Bowker (2003: 168) writes: 'Lydia was horrified by unfolding events. To her, Eric Blair did not seem good enough for Eileen – rather seedy and unattractive, she thought, hardly the man her delightful friend deserved.'

Funder goes on to claim none of the biographers makes it clear that it was Eileen who made sure that the clergyman at their wedding left out the 'obey' clause (p. 71). But Bowker writes (2003; 189): 'When the vows came to be read, Eileen, it seems had arranged with John Woods [the clergyman] to omit one of the promises. Orwell wrote to his old love Brenda [Salkeld] the following day: "We were married yesterday in correct style at the parish church but not with the correct marriage service as the clergyman left out the 'obey' clause among other things."'

STRESS ON HOMOSEXUALITY ALSO PROBLEMATIC

Funder's stress on Orwell's misogyny 'as a code for homosexuality' and his 'virulent homosexuality' (p. 88) is problematic too. As in many aspects of his personality Orwell's attitudes to homosexuals were complex, ambivalent and contradictory. In a number of places in his writings Orwell attacked homosexuals in appalling, homophobic language, most infamously in *The Road to Wigan Pier*: 'You and I and the editor of the *Times Lit Supp* and the Nancy poets and the Archbishop of Canterbury and Comrade X, author of *Marxism for Infants* – all of us really owe the comparative decency of our lives to poor drudges underground, blackened to the eyes, with their throats full of coal dust, driving their shovels forward with arms and belly muscles of steel' (1980 [1937]: 138-139). When approached by Nancy Cunard to contribute to her *Authors Take Sides on the Spanish Civil War*, Orwell's response is 'one of the most intemperate paragraphs he ever committed to paper', according to D.J. Taylor (2003: 245): 'Will you please stop sending me this bloody rubbish. … I am not one of your fashionable pansies like Auden and Spender…'

But in *Down and Out in Paris and London*, at a time when homosexuality was illegal, he deals with the subject quite openly

RICHARD LANCE KEEBLE

and in an understanding way (Keeble 2019: 91). For instance, when reflecting on his experiences, Orwell argues that one of the 'great evils' of the tramp's life is that he is cut off entirely from contact with women (1980 [1933]: 115). He continues: 'It is obvious what results of this must be: homosexuality, for instance, and occasional rape cases. … The sexual impulse, not to put it any higher, is a fundamental impulse, and starvation of it can be almost as demoralizing as physical hunger' (ibid). Many of his friends and colleagues were homosexuals. In the case of Kay Dick (who later went on to write a dystopian novel *They*, in 1977) he went out of his way to support her launch of the *Windmill* journal in 1945 sending her his wonderful essay 'In defence of P.G. Wodehouse'.

A large section of *Wifedom* (pp 97-183) focuses on Orwell's time in Spain (quite soon after his marriage) fighting in a Republican militia (POUM) during the civil war – and his failure to mention by name Eileen who came to join him at the front and worked tirelessly for the Independent Labour Party in Barcelona. For Funder, Eileen remains scandalously 'invisible' throughout. 'Orwell mentions "my wife" thirty-seven times. … not once is Eileen named. No character can come to life without a name. But from a wife, which is a job description, it can all be stolen' (p. 181). Yet according to Jeffrey Meyers (2023), after being convicted of treason and condemned to death, Orwell 'feared he could be murdered by Soviet agents whom he knew were operating in England, and wanted to *protect* Eileen from dangerous reprisals by hiding her connection to POUM'.

INVISIBLE: PREVIOUS FEMINIST CRITIQUES

For her part, Funder fails to acknowledge previous feminist Orwellian critiques (so in her own way making them 'invisible') such as Anne K. Mellor's 'Orwell's view of women' (1983), Daphne Patai's *The Orwell Mystique: A Study in Male Ideology* (1984), Deirdre Beddoe's essay 'Hindrance and help-meets: Women in the writings of George Orwell' (1984), and Beatrix Campbell's *Wigan Pier Revisited* (1984a) and 'Orwell: Paterfamilias or Big Brother?' (1984b).

She echoes biographer Sylvia Topp in arguing that Eileen's input was crucial in the writing of *Animal Farm*: 'The form of the book itself – a fable, novel, satire – was Eileen's idea. She steered him away from writing a critical essay on Stalin and totalitarianism and then, in bed to stay warm while the bombs fell, they worked on it together. In *Animal Farm* her psychological depth and sympathy met his political insights and made a masterpiece' (p. 292). But earlier she failed to acknowledge the influence of Eileen (a paid-up member of the Peace Pledge Union) on his outspoken pacifism during the lead-up to the Second World War (see Keeble 2020).

Funder also misses a number of fascinating 'As I Please' columns Orwell wrote for *Tribune* between 1943 and 1947 which, it could be argued, bear the distinct imprint of Eileen's influence. On 28 April 1944, Orwell followed up the comments of Basil Henriques, chairman of the East London juvenile court, who had attacked girls of 14 for dressing and talking like those of 18 and 19 and putting 'filth and muck on their faces' (Anderson 2006: 132). The polymath Orwell, no doubt assisted by Eileen, proceeded to offer, in around 1,000 words, a potted history of women's make-up, no less. In another column, responding to a reader's letter, he used a serious critique of women's papers (not normally considered worthy of attention by either the media or academia at the time) – such as *Lucky Star*, the *Golden Star* and *Peg's Paper* – to explore the ways in which press proprietors and the ruling class in general promote the notion of the moral superiority of the poor as 'the deadliest form of escapism' (*CWGO* XVI: 305). In 1945, Orwell reviewed Virginia Woolf's seminal feminist text, *A Room of One's Own*, 'a discussion of the handicaps which have prevented women, as compared with men, from producing literature of the first order'. There is no condemnation. Rather, he suggests that 'almost anyone of the male sex could read it with advantage' (Newsinger 2018: 134-135). In another *Tribune* column, on 8 November 1946, Orwell deconstructed in remarkable detail a copy of the American fashion magazine *Vogue* (sent to him because it carried a profile of the celebrated author of *Animal Farm*). So, in the process of studying a women's journal (elsewhere largely dismissed as popular trivia), cheap women's journals and the mass media in general, Orwell in effect invents the discipline of Cultural Studies.

ORWELL'S DECISION TO LEAVE ADOPTED SON AND EILEEN AND HEAD FOR CONTINENT: THE DEBATE CONTINUES

Orwell's decision to head off to the Continent to report on the final days of the Second World War for the *Observer* and *Manchester Evening News* just a few months after he and Eileen had adopted the baby Richard is difficult to understand. Funder blames Orwell for leaving his sick wife and she dismisses his reporting as 'unimportant' (p. 341). But there are complications. Orwell himself was very sick (though Funder does not acknowledge this). While staying at Hôtel Scribe, in Paris, along with the international press corps, he spent most of his time in bed. He was even in hospital in Cologne when he received news of Eileen's death under anaesthetic during an operation at a Newcastle hospital.

The fact that Orwell has gone to the Continent as a war correspondent in 1945 – when clearly in poor health – having been rejected for military service on two previous occasions on

RICHARD LANCE KEEBLE

account of his poor health raises even more questions. Perhaps he was hoping to earn some money to finance the family's move to the remote Scottish island of Jura. Perhaps he was doing some kind of intelligence work (a crucial part he may have considered of the war effort) for his close friend and *Observer* journalist David Astor, whose intelligence ties went back to 1939. Significantly all the men he met in Paris (Malcolm Muggeridge, 'Freddie' Ayer, Ernest Hemingway, Harold Acton) had intelligence links and according to Stephen Dorril, in his history of MI6, Orwell attended a conference of the Committee for European Freedom on behalf of Astor (2000: 456-457). Perhaps this helps explain how Orwell could evade this time the health checks required for all war correspondents.

There is, for some reason, no Index in *Wifedom* to assist the reader.

CONCLUDING REFLECTION

Just as Funder was completing her researches, *George Orwell Studies* published Angela Smith's excellent paper on 'The important place of Sunderland Church High School in understanding Eileen O'Shaughnessy' (Vol 7, No. 1 pp 6-22) so crucially filling in the gaps about her pre-university education left by previous biographers. And reflecting the impact of Topp's biography, D.J. Taylor, in his *Orwell: The New Life* (2023), massively expands his coverage of Eileen. I look forward to more biographies (with far fewer fundamental flaws) of some of the other powerful women in Orwell's life.

REFERENCES

Anderson, Paul (2006) *Orwell in* Tribune, London: Politico's

Beddoe, Deirdre (1984) Hindrance and help-meets: Women in the writings of George Orwell, Norris, Chistopher (ed.) *Inside the Myth: Orwell: Views from the Left*, London: Lawrence & Wishart pp 139-152

Bowker, Gordon (2003) *George Orwell*, London: Little, Brown

Brooks, Richard (2023) Sadistic and misogynistic? Row erupts over sex claims in book about George Orwell's marriage, *Guardian*, 11 November. Available online at https://www.theguardian.com/books/2023/nov/11/row-sex-claims-book-george-orwell-marriage, accessed on 5 January 2024

Campbell, Beatrix (1984a) *Wigan Pier Revisited*, London: Virago

Campbell, Beatrix (1984b) Orwell: Paterfamilias or Big Brother?, Norris, Christopher (ed.) *Inside the Myth: Orwell: Views from the Left*, London: Lawrence & Wishart pp 128-136

Clarke, Ben (2016) George Orwell, Jack Hilton and the working class, *The Review of English Studies*, Vol. 67, No. 281 pp 764-785

Crick, Bernard (1980) *George Orwell: A Life*, Harmondsworth, Middlesex: Penguin

Davison, Peter (ed.) (2013 [2010]) *George Orwell: A Life in Letters*, London: Penguin

Dorril, Stephen (2000) *MI6: Fifty Years of Special Operations*, London: Fourth Estate

Garréta, Anne F. (1996) In light of invisibility, *French Studies*, Vol. 90 pp 205-213. Available online at https://www.jstor.org/stable/2930364

Keeble, Richard Lance (2019) Beyond the dystopian gloom: Orwell and sexuality, Joseph, Sue and Keeble, Richard Lance (eds) *Sex and Journalism: Critical, Global Perspectives*, London: Bite-Sized Books pp 88-96

Keeble, Richard Lance (2020) Orwell, Eileen and anti-militarism, Orwell Society website, 20 May. Available online at https://orwellsociety.com/eileen-orwell-and-anti-militarism/

Keeble, Richard Lance (2023) The Wigan Diary celebrated, Orwell Society website, 23 June. Available online at https://orwellsociety.com/the-wigan-diary-celebrated/

Mellor, Anne K. (1983) 'You're only a rebel from the waist downward': Orwell's view on women, Stansky, Peter (ed.) *On Nineteen Eighty-Four*, Stanford, California: Standford Alumni Association pp 115-125

Meyers, Jeffrey (2000) *Orwell: Wintry Conscience of a Generation*, New York: W.W. Norton & Co.

Meyers, Jeffrey (2023) In defence of George Orwell, thearticle.com, 17 September. Available online at https://www.thearticle.com/in-defence-of-george-orwell?fbclid=IwAR0x1lk4Dst2AuXc08GioRg0G_tydcMFWUJvSgKTogQ6rd4MZMpDf4gM4Pw

Newsinger, John (2018) *Hope Lies in the Proles: George Orwell and the Left*, London: Pluto Press

Orwell, George (1980 [1933]) *Down and Out in Paris and London, Collected Non-Fiction: Complete and Unabridged*, London: Secker & Warburg/Octopus pp 15-120

Orwell, George (1980 [1937]) *The Road to Wigan Pier, Collected Non-Fiction*, London: Secker & Warburg/Octopus pp 123-231

Orwell, George (1998) *The Complete Works of George Orwell (CWGO)*, XX Vols, Davison, Peter (ed.) London: Secker & Warburg

Orwell, Sonia and Angus, Ian (1970) *The Collected Essays, Journalism and Letters of George Orwell (CEJL), Vol I: An Age Like This*, Harmondsworth, Middlesex: Penguin

Taylor, D.J. (2003) *Orwell: The Life*, London: Chatto & Windus

Taylor, D.J. (2023) *Orwell: The New Life*, London: Constable

Richard Lance Keeble, Professor of Journalism at the University of Lincoln, was chair of The Orwell Society 2013-2020.

AND FINALLY

A new, lively diary item to intrigue and entertain Orwellians.

How much of what is written about George Orwell is written from an assumption? In her 2023 book *George Orwell and Russia*, Masha Karp points out that Myfanwy Westrope wrote to Bernard Crick when he had announced he had been appointed Orwell biographer. The Westropes owned Booklovers' Corner in Hampstead and employed George Orwell, Reg Groves, Jon Kimche and others in the 'thirties. Crick did not respond to her letter for four years by which time she had died. Perhaps he thought either Myfanwy or her husband, Francis, was like Mr McKechnie in *Keep the Aspidistra Flying*, although he must have known of the letter Orwell had written to Victor Gollancz saying there was no similarity. In fact, Myfanwy Westrope had seen Bolshevik Russia at first hand and many of those she corresponded with only just escaped being jailed there: while she was no Trotskyist it was unsurprising that Reg Groves, a founding member of the Balham Group of Trotskyists (see https://www.marxists.org/history/etol/document/balham/bg04.htm), found Booklovers' Corner a congenial place to work. Crick, it seems, could not imagine a woman of such political gravitas and felt no urgency about contacting her.

***

One of New Pitcher's privileges of 2023 was to assist in the salvation of the papers of the late Ian Angus from his Georgian house in Hampstead. Most original documents have gone to the Orwell Archive at University College London, others to the care of the Orwell Society. Lying open on a bookcase was *The Times Literary Supplement* of 15 September 1972, containing 'The Freedom of the Press' – Orwell's Introduction to *Animal Farm* re-discovered by Ian Angus.

***

What are we still missing? The Bertrand Russell Society are searching for letters between Russell and Orwell that Sonia Orwell once saw and tried to find again, unsuccessfully. Meanwhile, the Orwell Memorial Team in Huesca would like to find the marked-up copy of *Homage to Catalonia* that Orwell left with Roger Senhouse. It was sight of this copy that led Professor Peter Davison to make his changes to the book in the *Complete Works* edition, moving some chapters to Appendices as Orwell intended should the book be reprinted in his lifetime. Senhouse died in the 1970s and his library was sold. Given Peter Davison thanks a 'George Locke' for sight of the copy, this was probably the man who dealt in rare books, especially science fiction, as 'Ferret Fantasy'. Locke, though, was a dealer and the book moved on as have his records. Does anyone have an idea where the marked-up copy may be now?

***

Beasts of England, Adam Biles's re-writing of Orwell's *Animal Farm* (reviewed in this issue of *GOS* by Douglas Kerr), was published last September by one of our smaller and more adventurous publishers, the Norwich-based Galley Beggar, who took pre-orders. Copies arrived tissue-wrapped and bound with ribbons – if New Pitcher's heirs are to inherit anything how can he read it without reducing its value?

***

Well done Thomas McGrath, who examined four possible lodgings in Wigan where Orwell may have stayed as he researched the plight of the poor and unemployed in early 1936: 72 Warrington Lane, 22 Darlington Street, 35 Sovereign Road and 72 Darlington Street. While McGrath found that Orwell stayed in only two it remains unclear which two of the four they were. See https://ifthosewallscouldtalk.wordpress.com/2023/08/14/long-lost-histories-george-orwells-lodgings-wigan/. When Bernard Crick, Orwell's biographer, visited the town, as part of his investigations he sought information from folk queueing in a fish and chip shop. But like McGrath he did not come up with any clear idea of where precisely Orwell stayed.

***

An exercise New Pitcher thinks he saw or heard somewhere: *Down and Out in Paris and London*, particularly the Parisian section, deals with only a short period of Orwell's residence in the French capital. Firstly, how short? And secondly, what was he doing the rest of the time? Perhaps the researches of Masha Karp (again), Darcy Moore and Duncan Roberts (author of *Orwell à Paris*) will give us a more detailed chronology.

***

A question for trivia fiends: who were Joyce Pritchard and Gladys M. Blackburn? Answer: they were the nurse and housekeeper at Greystone, the home of Gwen O'Shaughnessy in Stockton-on-Tees, where Eileen and Orwell went with their new baby. And Joyce Pritchard and Gladys M. Blackburn were the witnesses to Eileen's will. So this raises a new question: was Eileen so weak even before her operation in March 1945 (which was to prove fatal) that she could not travel into Sunderland or Newcastle to sign the will and have it witnessed in a solicitor's office?

George Orwell Studies

Subscription information
Each volume contains two issues, published half-yearly.

Annual Subscription (including postage)

Personal Subscription

UK	£45
Europe	£50
RoW	£55

Institutional Subscription

UK	£100
Europe	£115
RoW	£120

Single Issue copies can be purchased (subject to availability)

Enquiries regarding subscriptions and orders should be sent to:

> Journals Fulfilment Department
> Abramis Academic
> ASK House
> Northgate Avenue
> Bury St Edmunds
> Suffolk, IP32 6BB
> UK

Tel: +44(0)1284 717884
Email: info@abramis.co.uk

www.ingramcontent.com/pod-product-compliance
Lightning Source LLC
Chambersburg PA
CBHW080747300426
44114CB00019B/2671